Library of
Davidson College

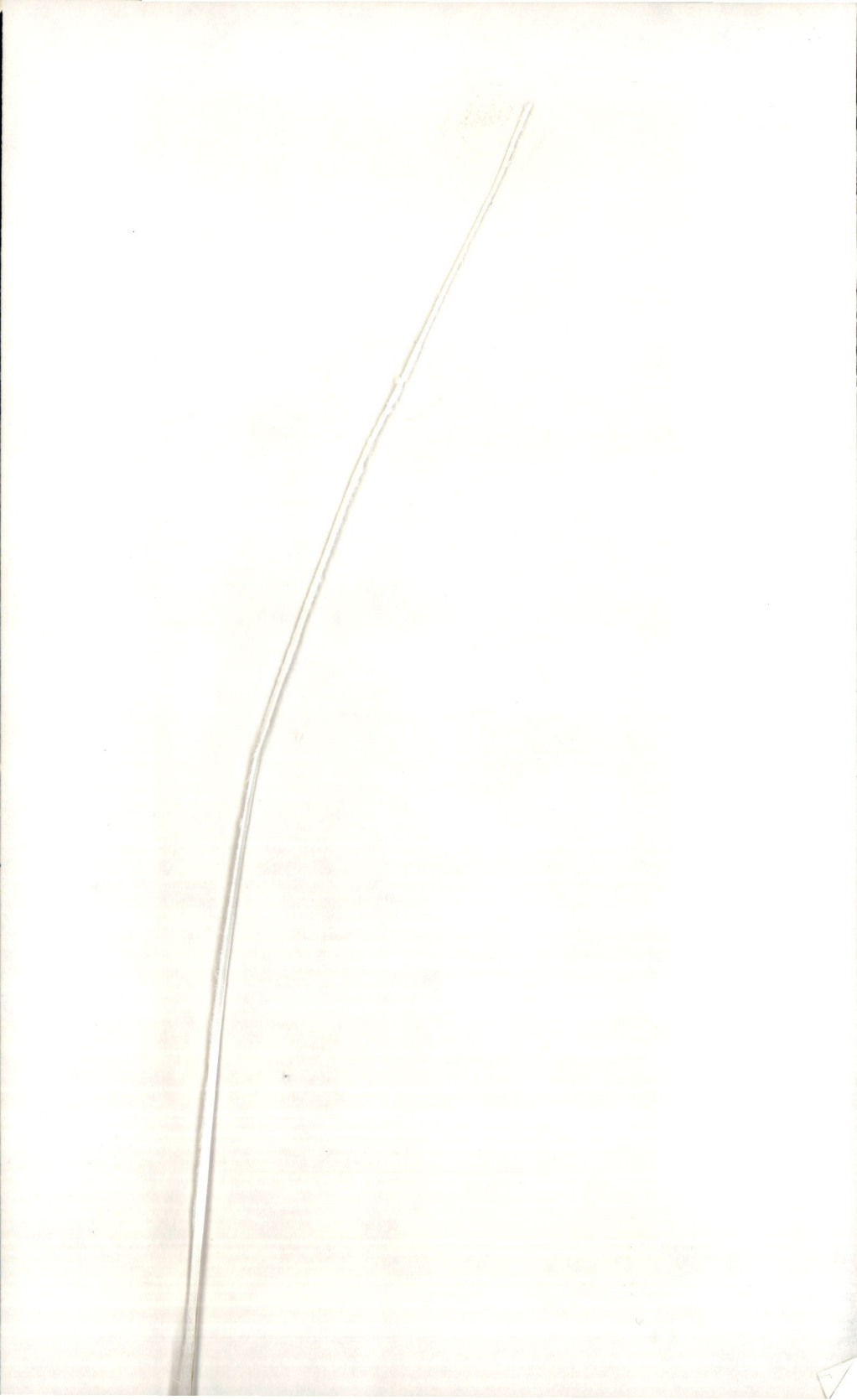

Conventional War
and Escalation

Conventional War and Escalation: The Soviet View

Joseph D. Douglass, Jr.

and

Amoretta M. Hoeber

Published by

Crane, Russak & Company, Inc.
New York

National Strategy Information Center, Inc.

**Conventional War and Escalation:
The Soviet View**

Published in the United States by

Crane, Russak & Company, Inc.
3 East 44th Street
New York, NY 10017

Copyright © 1981 National Strategy Information Center, Inc.
111 East 58th Street
New York, NY 10022

Library of Congress Cataloging in Publication Data

Douglass, Joseph D.
Conventional war and escalation.

(Strategy papers ; 37)
1. Soviet Union—Military policy. 2. Warfare, Conventional.
3. Atomic warfare. I. Hoeber, Amoretta M. II. Title III. Series.
UA770.D65   355'.033047   81-3265
ISBN 0-8448-1390-7 (pbk.)   AACR2

No part of this publication may be reproduced,
stored in a retrieval system, or transmitted
in any form or by any means, electronic,
mechanical, photocopying, recording,
or otherwise, without the prior
written permission of the publisher.

Printed in the United States of America

Contents

I. *Introduction*   1
II. *The Soviet Interest in Conventional Capabilities*   9
     Response to U.S./NATO Strategy Shifts   10
     Non-Nuclear Unit and Subunit Operations   11
     Non-Nuclear War   13
     Summary Statement of the Soviet Interest in Conventional Capabilities   14
III. *Advantages of Beginning a War with a Conventional Phase*   17
IV. *Characteristics of a Conventional Phase*   25
     A Conventional Phase "Under Threat of Nuclear Use"   25
     Characteristic Features of a Conventional Phase   31
     Specific Tasks   36
V. *Transition to Nuclear Operations*   41
     When to Strike   45
     Considerations of Self-Deterrence   51
     Escalation Flexibility   58

Preface

In recent years a number of Western analysts have supported the notion that the Soviets, having come to agree with the West that nuclear war is impossible, are undergoing a shift away from nuclear and toward conventional doctrine and strategy. In this study, the authors review a large body of evidence from the Soviet military literature of the 1960s and 1970s, and conclude that no such shift in interest from nuclear toward conventional war in Europe can be identified either in Soviet military writings or in their force improvements.

Douglass and Hoeber show that while "the Soviets have clearly and continually recognized the need to be able to conduct non-nuclear war," such capabilities are geared "primarily for fighting specific types of wars which are expected to remain non-nuclear, and for exploitation and occupations in the context of nuclear war." The primary Soviet force development objective continues to focus on flexible combined arms capabilities. While the Soviets do acknowledge the possibility that a major war might begin with conventional warfare, such a beginning is regarded as only a phase, which would be used (by either side) to better prepare for the subsequent, more important, and potentially decisive nuclear portion of the war.

In reviewing the Soviet literature, the authors find that in practically every respect, Soviet concepts differ markedly from the perceptions of those concepts (to the extent they are treated at all) most often encountered in Western writings. In fact, concepts and related discussions contained in Soviet works often appear to be simply overlooked, not addressed, or discounted as mere rhetoric by the West. In their delineation and assessment of Soviet views on conventional capabilities and escalation, Douglass and Hoeber place emphasis on those aspects which seem most subject to the gap between Western perceptions and the apparent Soviet reality, and thus make a significant contribution toward enhancing Western understanding of Soviet military thinking.

The Soviets assume that major war in nearly all cases will either begin with nuclear strikes or become nuclear as the conflict progresses. Within the context of this tenet of Soviet thinking, the authors engage in a

Preface

careful and thoroughly documented analysis of the Soviet approach to conventional capabilities and operations, and the relationship of conventional conflict to nuclear war. The major topics addressed in this monograph include: Soviet interests in conventional capabilities (in particular, sub-unit operations); the advantages which might be derived from a conventional phase (most of which are oriented toward better achievement of an effective, surprise nuclear strike); the characteristics of a conventional phase; and the factors that bear on the timing of the transition to nuclear operations.

Joseph D. Douglass, Jr. is currently Scientific Advisor at IRT Corporation, in McLean, Virginia. His previous positions include Director of the Policy and Strategy Analysis Division, System Planning Corporation; Deputy Director of the Tactical Technology Office, Defense Advanced Research Projects Agency; and posts with the Institute for Defense Analyses, the Research Triangle Institute, and Sandia Corporation. He was educated at Cornell University, where he received the B.E.E., M.S., and Ph.D. degrees, the latter specializing in network theory and applied mathematics. Dr. Douglass is the author of numerous articles and books, among them *Soviet Military Strategy in Europe* (Pergamon, 1980), *Soviet Strategy for Nuclear War* (Hoover Institution Press, 1979, co-authored with Amoretta M. Hoeber), and *The Soviet Theater Nuclear Offensive* (USGPO, 1976).

During the writing of this study, Amoretta M. Hoeber was on the professional staff of System Planning Corporation, Arlington, Virginia. She has since been appointed Deputy Assistant Secretary of the Army for Research and Development. Ms. Hoeber previously was Director of the Department of Military Policy Analysis at General Research Corporation, and a member of the research staffs of the Rand Corporation, Analytic Services, Inc., and the Stanford Research Institute. She received the A.B. degree from Stanford University, and has done graduate studies in mathematics at Stanford, American University, and UCLA. Her publications include *The Chemistry of Defeat* (Institute for Foreign Policy Analysis, 1981), a chapter in *The United States in the 1980s* (Hoover Institution Press, 1980, co-authored with J. D. Douglass, Jr.), and *Selected Readings from Soviet Military Thought (1963–1973)* (USGPO, forthcoming, with J. D. Douglass, Jr.).

                Frank R. Barnett, *President*
                National Strategy Information Center, Inc.

October 1981

I. Introduction

Over the past decade considerable Western attention has been focused on what has been termed a relatively rapid growth in Soviet interest in, and capabilities for, conducting conventional war in Europe. The evidence cited to support this interpretation includes statements in the Soviet literature regarding the need to be able to fight without nuclear weapons; Warsaw Pact exercises wherein nuclear weapons were not employed early in the conflict; and, perhaps most concretely, increases in inventories of Soviet conventional equipment, such as tactical aircraft, artillery, armored personnel carriers, etc. Accepting this interpretation, former Secretary of Defense James R. Schlesinger in 1974 cited the exercise aspect:

> In their exercises the Soviets have indicated far greater interest in the notions of controlled nuclear war and nonnuclear war than has ever before been reflected in Soviet doctrine. As I indicated earlier, I think the doctrine is undergoing change.[1]

Former Secretary of Defense Donald H. Rumsfeld in 1976 referred to both the equipment and exercise changes:

> In the conventional area, the advent of self-propelled artillery, the BMP, and new air defense weapons provide great increases in firepower; the improvements in crew protection in artillery and APCs greatly decrease the risk to their soldiers. Overall, what is being seen is an effort that improved mobility, firepower, support, and protection for men and weapons, which are essential inputs to combat success.

---

1. *Nuclear Weapons and Foreign Policy.* Hearings before the Subcommittee on U.S. Security Agreements and Commitments Abroad and the Subcommittee on Arms Control, International Law and Organization of the Committee on Foreign Relations, United States Senate, Ninety-third Congress, 2nd Session, on U.S. Nuclear Weapons in Europe and U.S.-U.S.S.R. Strategic Doctrines and Policies; March 7, 14, and April 4, 1974; p. 183.

With these advances, the Soviets appear to have changed their exercise and training practices to emphasize longer periods of conventional conflict before escalating to a nuclear environment.[2]

In more recent Posture Statements, former Secretary of Defense Harold Brown has also discussed the improvements, referring to them in the sections on conventional capabilities.[3]

Unfortunately, statements such as these (which receive considerable public exposure and discussion) tend to reflect U.S. rather than Soviet thinking and planning, and do not fully convey what changes in fact are taking place. At the heart of this problem is the systems analysis approach commonly utilized in the United States, with its overriding emphasis on categorization. Characterizations of the Soviet posture and Soviet policies contained in the types of sources cited above thus are a) focused on areas relevant to U.S. procurement issues (i.e., comparative hardware and technology[4] rather than force use [doctrine and strategy]); and b) considered within the categorizations applicable to U.S. forces. Hence, the threat posed by the Soviet Union is divided into three categories: strategic nuclear, theater nuclear, and conventional. Sometimes discussions regarding the theater nuclear and conventional components, while separate, are at least located next to one another within a general purpose section; at other times, the theater nuclear and strategic nuclear aspects may be combined as simply nuclear. However, for the most part, U.S. statements contain three separate discussions, with very little consideration of the interactions which occur between the force

---

2. Report of Secretary of Defense Donald H. Rumsfeld to the Congress on the Fiscal Year 1977 Budget and Its Implications for the Fiscal Year 1978 Authorization Request and the Fiscal Year 1977–1981 Defense Programs; January 27, 1976; p. 98.

3. Harold Brown, Secretary of Defense, *Department of Defense Annual Report, Fiscal Year 1979,* February 2, 1978, pp. 75–76; and Harold Brown, Secretary of Defense, *Department of Defense Annual Report, Fiscal Year 1981,* January 29, 1980, p. 102.

4. In this regard, see also the strong technology focus of the recent *Adelphi Papers* entitled "New Conventional Weapons and East-West Security," *Adelphi Papers #144 and #145* (London: The International Institute for Strategic Studies, 1978).

Introduction

categories. Thus, for example, U.S. discussions only recently have begun to include an assessment of the contribution to theater nuclear warfare made by conventional equipment, such as that referred to earlier.

Although the above-described categorization approach may correctly reflect Western patterns of thinking and acquisition planning, certain problems are generated when discussions of the Warsaw Pact threat are organized in the same manner, since the Soviet Union and its allies appear to employ a different organizational mode. Indeed, the essence of the Warsaw Pact approach is combined-arms combat—a concept which is, for the most part, lost in or absent from the Western classification scheme of strategic nuclear, theater nuclear, and conventional components. Many analysts in the West have a tendency to interpret the notion of combined-arms combat as belonging to the conventional realm. In the sharply contrasting Soviet approach, however, combined-arms is the combination of all forces and all means used to their maximum advantage to achieve victory. Of first and foremost importance to the Soviets in modern times is the combination of nuclear strike plus maneuver, as defined by Lt. General V. Reznichenko in *Voyennaya mysl'*[5] in 1973:

> Combined-arms combat began to be viewed as a combination of nuclear

---

5. This journal is the official military-theoretical organ of the Soviet Ministry of Defense (see William F. Scott, *Soviet Sources of Military Doctrine and Strategy* [New York: Crane, Russak & Co., 1975]), and is also regarded as the official organ of the Soviet General Staff. It is a restricted, or classified, journal, written for senior officers of the Soviet armed forces, and is not usually available to Western analysts. The journal is believed to be authoritative and designed mainly for internal Soviet use; hence, it can be considered less subject to propaganda or disinformation directed toward the West than those Soviet journals and newspapers that are routinely received in the West. Additionally, *Voyennaya mysl'* is believed to be of special importance because it is one of the few Soviet journals in which problems and issues of military strategy are regularly examined by senior military and party officials for other senior military officers. Approximately 9,000 translated pages from the 1960s and 1970s have been recently declassified in the United States, allowing open discussion of their contents and the implications thereof.

strikes and maneuver emphasizing actions by large units, units, and subunits of various arms and services coordinated in objective, time, and place.[6]

The keystone nature of this combination is clearly evident in another important Soviet work, the *Dictionary of Basic Military Terms*. Consider, for example, the following definitions of "combat," "combined-arms battle," "engagement," and "offensive operations," which tend to span the spectrum of the various levels of conflict that might comprise general purpose force operations:

> *Combat:* An organized clash of combatant units with the enemy, using strikes and fire of all types, for the purpose of achieving victory.[7]
>
> *Combined-Arms Battle:* A battle fought by a combined-arms formation (or unit) together with its attached formations (or units) of other service branches and aviation; and in maritime sectors, with naval forces as well. The use of nuclear weapons and the participation of the various service branches (or forces), in conjunction with the great mobility of the troops, impart an especially decisive and maneuver-oriented character to a combined-arms battle.[8]
>
> *Engagement:* The aggregate of nuclear strikes and battles, united by a common operational concept, and conducted in one or several sectors simultaneously or sequentially.[9]
>
> *Offensive Operations:* The aggregate of nuclear strikes, coordinated and interrelated with regard to target, time and place, and the vigorous, offensive actions of the troops of a front (or an army), accomplished in accordance with a unified concept for the attainment of operational or strategic goals.[10]

A second dimension of U.S. conceptualization that may unduly bias the interpretation of the evidence on Soviet capabilities and strategy is

---

6. Lt. Gen. V. Reznichenko, "Tactics—A Component Part of the Art of Warfare," *Voyennaya mysl'*, No. 12, December 1973, FPD 0048, August 20, 1974, p. 40.

7. *Dictionary of Basic Military Terms* (A Soviet View) (Moscow: 1965), translated and published under the auspices of the U.S. Air Force, Soviet Military Thought Series No. 9 (Washington, D.C.: U.S. Government Printing Office, 1976), p. 27.

8. *Ibid.*, p. 137.

9. *Ibid.*, p. 206.

10. *Ibid.*, p. 131.

Introduction

the view that nuclear war is basically impossible and that nuclear weapons are hence not employable, particularly in the theater. This position was clearly stated in Congressional testimony by former Assistant Secretary of Defense Paul C. Warnke in 1974:

> The time has passed for infatuation with nuclear weapons as the key to security. The decades since the 1950s have shown that they are largely unusable and serve largely to see to it that the other side can't use its nuclear weapons. NATO has never been able to develop a military strategy which would utilize even a few of the tactical nuclear weapons we maintain at its disposal.
>
> NATO's deterrent efficacy is dependent in part on tactical nuclear weapons, but the role of these weapons is largely theoretical.[11]

Also in Congressional testimony, former Assistant Secretary of Defense Alain C. Enthoven has stated:

> Two-sided tactical nuclear war makes no sense at all . . . tactical nuclear weapons cannot defend Europe, they can only destroy it. . . . beyond the limited demonstrative use of a few weapons, there is no such thing as tactical nuclear war in the sense of sustained purposive military operations.[12]

The same thrusts and conclusions which are characteristic of this position can be discerned in the Fiscal Year 1979 Department of Defense Posture Statement. For example:

> There is no evidence that nuclear firepower can substitute for the other elements of a conventional capability. Nor is it at all clear that anything approximating a traditional military campaign could be fought with nuclear weapons.
>
> . . . The U.S. theater nuclear forces have a symbolic importance that transcends their direct military value.[13]

While the potential for escalation to nuclear war in the theater is treated more seriously than previously in the Fiscal Year 1981 Posture

---

11. U.S. Senate, *Nuclear Weapons and Foreign Policy*, p. 65.
12. Ibid., pp. 73–74.
13. Brown, *Department of Defense Annual Report, Fiscal Year 1979*, pp. 67–68.

Statement,[14] neither the contribution of conventional capabilities to nuclear war nor the Soviet concept of combined arms combat is addressed. The difference between the Western and Soviet concepts of war still appears to prevent the West from recognizing the totality of the role of conventional forces in Soviet strategy. The Soviet view of theater nuclear war involves battlefield *warfighting*, rather than merely a mass retaliatory nuclear strike, as usually conceived in the West. The Soviet emphasis on the combination of nuclear strike plus maneuver forces is the rationale presented in the Soviet literature for exactly those equipment improvements most often cited in the West as evidence of growing Soviet interest in conventional war. Self-propelled artillery, the BMP, air defense weapons, and advanced APCs are all explicitly singled out as being of crucial importance for surviving and operating (fighting and exploiting) in a nuclear environment. Even though it is quite true that these pieces of equipment obviously improve Soviet conventional capability, to assume that they have solely that function or that they evidence a shift in Soviet interest overlooks their essentiality for *fighting* a nuclear war (as opposed to merely retaliating).

Over the past several years the authors of this monograph have examined much of the evidence which has been used to support the notion that the Soviets, having come to agree with the West that nuclear war is impossible, are undergoing a shift in doctrine and strategy away from nuclear and toward conventional. In our analysis we have focused on the views and approach of the Soviet Union with respect to the conventional phase. The conclusions we have reached, several of which are considerably at variance with the "conventional wisdom," are:

1. No noticeable *shift* in interest from nuclear toward conventional war in Europe can be identified either in the Soviet military literature or in their force improvements. The Soviets have clearly and continuously recognized the need to be able to conduct non-nuclear war, but primarily for fighting specific types of wars which are expected to remain non-nuclear, and for exploitation and occupation operations in the context of nuclear war.

2. The basic character of the threat facing Western Europe today is

---

14. Brown, *Department of Defense Annual Report, Fiscal Year 1981*, pp. 91–96.

Introduction

neither newly conventional nor solely conventional. The main development in the Soviet posture over the past decade appears to be the emergence of an effective nuclear combined-arms *offensive* capability.

3. Should a war in Europe, in particular, or against the United States anywhere, begin with a conventional phase, Soviet operations planning would be conducted with the possible sudden transition to nuclear operations as *the* primary consideration. A conventional phase is viewed as one variant for the beginning of war; it constitutes only a phase, not the war itself. In the Soviet view, such a major war is likely to go nuclear, and it is probable that the nuclear phase will be decisive and will determine the course and outcome of the conflict. Therefore, the conventional phase is to be designed and conducted with transition to nuclear operations clearly the dominant concern. Hence, operations during conventional conflict may well take on certain characteristics of those during nuclear conflict.

4. In the Soviet view, the main advantages of an opening conventional phase lie in the fact that it permits the more effective implementation of a surprise nuclear strike if NATO forces already have been alerted and dispersed. Several advantages flowing from an initial conventional phrase are explicitly discussed in the Warsaw Pact military literature; all are associated with the problems of beginning a war with nuclear strike. An initial conventional phase is seen as a mechanism that provides the opportunity a) to solve problems of mobilization, force deployment and readiness, force dispersal, target acquisition, and airborne unit insertions, and b) to degrade NATO nuclear capabilities.

5. In general, the Soviet approach seems to be focused on determining the "most favorable time" to make the transition to nuclear operations. As identified in the Soviet literature, that time appears to be when a Soviet breakthrough first appears imminent. A number of particular factors, all of which seem to peak very early in the conventional phase, are prominent in the discussions of when to go nuclear. First, the assessment of the potential effectiveness of the strike must be favorable, meaning mainly that the targets have been identified and confirmed, and that the strike systems are ready. Second, the first strategic echelon forces should be in position to exploit the results of the strike. Third, initial operations, such as mass reconnaissance and insertion of airborne assault and intelligence units, should have been completed. Fourth, the initial phase of wartime mobilization should be under

way or in some cases have been completed (for example, in the case of the second strategic echelon). The commitment of second echelon and reserve units, itself a "culminating" moment of the offensive, is often linked to the initiation of nuclear operations. Surprise, a dominant factor in modern Soviet strategy, is especially important, and the drive to successfully achieve surprise tends to advance the timing of the nuclear decision. With these factors in mind, and making every effort to anticipate NATO moves, the Soviets would aim to preempt with an initial nuclear strike.

The impression gained from Soviet literature is that, in practically every respect, Soviet concepts differ markedly from the perceptions of those concepts (to the extent they are treated at all) most often encountered in Western literature. In fact, concepts and related discussions contained in Soviet works often appear to be simply overlooked, not addressed, or discounted as mere rhetoric by the West. Consequently, we have attempted to structure the material in the following analysis not only to bring out the Soviet view itself, but also to illuminate the differences between Soviet thinking in various topic areas and the corresponding U.S. perceptions of that thinking. Thus, emphasis in this paper is placed on those aspects of the threat which we see as most subject to this gap between Western perceptions and the apparent Soviet reality: i.e., the degree of interest of the Soviet Union in having the ability to fight conventionally; the characteristic features of an initial conventional phase as seen by the Soviets; and the Soviet approach to making the transition to nuclear operations, including their concern for collateral damage.

II. The Soviet Interest in Conventional Capabilities

It is very difficult to establish the point in time when a particular concept actually emerges in Soviet military thought, if for no other reason than the limited availability of Soviet military literature in the West. In several independent analyses, however, it has been concluded that the possibility of a conventional opening phase was recognized in the Soviet literature at least as early as January 1964. For example, the following excerpt appeared in a *Voyennaya mysl'* article on augmentation in modern combat published in that month:

> . . . Under certain conditions of a war the strategic air force may be a most dependable and effective means of augmentation of strategic efforts. This may be especially true when the enemy has started the war without resorting to nuclear weapons. In such a case the augmentation of efforts will mainly take the same form as in past wars, by the use of conventional weapons.[15]

By mid-1964, the idea of being prepared for beginning warfare with a non-nuclear phase was appearing regularly in Soviet writings, and, by 1966, non-nuclear operations at the unit and subunit level were being exercised as part of the Warsaw Pact tactical repertoire.[16]

---

15. Maj. Gen. Kh. Dzhelaukhov, "The Augmentation of Strategic Efforts in Modern Arms Armed Conflict," *Voyennaya mysl'*, No. 1, January 1964, FDD 939, August 4, 1965, p. 25.

16. A former senior East European officer has stated that provision for a conventional variant was first incorporated into Warsaw Pact war plans in 1963. This conventional variant was, however, not for a major war. Rather, it was for small-scale Berlin-like actions, over which the Soviets believed the United States would not go to war, because of both a growing tendency toward isolationism in the U.S. and a trend toward autonomy in Europe. Any major conflict involving the United States was still regarded as likely to be nuclear and global in character. (Interviews with a former East European senior officer, October–December, 1978.)

The Soviet conventional interest appears to have stemmed from four factors: response to U.S./NATO strategy shifts, recognition of the need to conduct non-nuclear operations at the unit and subunit level, recognition of the need to be able to fight non-nuclear wars, and recognition of potential problems involved in starting an operation with a mass nuclear strike.

Response to U.S./NATO Strategy Shifts

A most obvious factor in the development of Soviet interest in conventional conflict was the U.S./NATO shift in doctrine from emphasis on massive nuclear retaliation to flexible response. From the Soviet point of view, the signals coming from the West in this regard were certainly very mixed, and the dynamics of action and reaction in this case are therefore quite complex. Following the inauguration of the new U.S. administration in 1961, the Soviets began to recognize that U.S. policy regarding NATO defense was changing. It is not known when the USSR arrived at this perception. However, there is reason to believe that Soviet attention to General Maxwell Taylor's book, *The Uncertain Trumpet*—which received widespread distribution in the Soviet Union in 1962, when 10,000 copies in translation were printed—may constitute an appropriate beginning. A 1966 *Voyennaya mysl'* article suggests that the shift in NATO strategy was clearly recognized in the Soviet Union by the middle of 1963.[17] This article makes particular reference to the December 1962 Nassau Conference between President Kennedy and British Prime Minister McMillan; at this meeting, the Skybolt missile was cancelled and Kennedy, according to the Soviet article, indicated that a shift in NATO strategy from nuclear to conventional was to take place.

At the same time, however, the U.S. nuclear buildup in Europe continued well into 1964–1965. It was not until close to the end of this period that the character of the U.S. nuclear forces in Europe began to change, with the removal of the Intermediate Range Ballistic Missiles (IRBMs) and the Davy Crockett, the displacement to the rear of some forward deployments, and the installation of permissive action link

---

17. Capt. Yu. Nepodayev, "On 'Nuclear Threshold' in NATO Strategy," *Voyennaya mysl'*, No. 6, June 1966, FPIR 0503/67, June 26, 1967.

(PAL) devices on the remaining nuclear warheads. Only with these changes did the forces begin to reflect the basic 1961 policy shift.

It is likely that the Kennedy-Khrushchev talks in the early 1960s on how to prevent accidental war also served as an input to the developing Soviet view of the U.S. policy shift. It is quite probable that the two leaders discussed the growing NATO emphasis on conventional strategy.[18] At any rate, the notion of the necessity of being able to respond conventionally to a possible conventional attack by NATO was clearly present in the Soviet literature by the mid-1960s.

While the purpose of the United States in undertaking such a policy shift was to alter the relative role and weight of nuclear and conventional arms (i.e., to raise the nuclear threshold), no such motivation has been identified in the Soviet literature. At best it can be said that a main task of Soviet military science is to study the doctrine, strategy, and tactics of the enemy in order to better understand how a war might begin, and thus to become better prepared to win it. It is in this vein that much of the Soviet discussion regarding a non-nuclear phase appears to be couched.

Non-Nuclear Unit and Subunit Operations

Concern was also emerging during the first half of the 1960s with respect to the need for Soviet forces at the unit and subunit level to be able to fight without recourse to nuclear weapons. In this connection, it is important to bear in mind that Soviet statements on the need to conduct non-nuclear operations at the unit and subunit level do not necessarily imply that a war will be exclusively conventional; rather, these statements can refer to either nuclear or non-nuclear contexts. For example, as stated by Marshal Grechko in 1971:

---

18. It has been reported that Premier Khrushchev stopped off in Prague on his way back from meeting with President Kennedy in Vienna in June, 1961. At that time, Khrushchev briefed President Novotny on the outcome of the summit meeting. Khrushchev indicated that Kennedy had brought up the shift to a conventional strategy in Europe. Khrushchev, however, at that time, stated to Novotny that he did not believe the shift was real and instead considered it to be a U.S. ruse to get the Soviet Union to stop producing missiles. (Interviews with a former East European senior officer, October–December, 1978.)

... in a future world war, if the imperialists start it, nuclear missiles will be the deciding means of warfare. Along with this conventional weapons will also find use, and under certain conditions, the units and subunits can conduct combat actions solely with conventional means.[19]

At least by the mid-1960s, the Soviets had recognized that they were becoming too dependent on nuclear weapons—i.e., nuclear weapons were being expected to do the whole job. (Perhaps this realization was underscored during the process of developing selected conventional variants in the war plans of the nation.) The Soviets began to realize that because nuclear weapons could not be counted on to do everything, it was essential for units and subunits to be able to fight with non-nuclear, as well as nuclear, weapons. Several reasons were put forth for not relying completely on nuclear weapons. First, nuclear weapons were a scarce commodity in the 1960s, and simply were not available in large quantities at the battlefield level. Hence, units and subunits might not have any nuclear weapons available for their use. Second, nuclear weapons were viewed as a primary target for the enemy, and the Soviets accordingly recognized that their nuclear armaments might well be destroyed by NATO. Consequently, under such circumstances, lower-level commands could not count on having nuclear weapons available. Third, because command and control was viewed as a primary target as well, severe disruptions in this regard were anticipated. For this reason, also, the Soviets considered it inexpedient for their forces to count on the availability of nuclear fire support.

Destructiveness was a further item of concern to the Soviets. They recognized that, in many cases, it would be *disadvantageous* to use nuclear weapons, in view of the resulting physical destruction and possible radioactive contamination which would pose problems for their own troop operations. Consequently, the Soviets concluded that it was essential for units and subunits (i.e., regiment level and below, which—incidentally—do not have organic nuclear fire support) to be able to conduct operations using only conventional means, since it might be judged inappropriate for nuclear weapons to be employed in the area in which the troops were operating.

---

19. A.A. Grechko, "On Guard for Peace and the Building of Communism," December 2, 1971, JPRS 45602, p. 43.

The Soviet Interest in Conventional Capabilities

Finally, it was recognized that while nuclear weapons are the decisive element in combat, ground force operations are absolutely essential for victory because only the latter can secure the final objective—namely, the destruction of the remaining elements of hostile military forces, the capture and occupation of the enemy's territory, and the installation of appropriate "realistic" governments. It is explicitly stated in *Voyennaya mysl'* that this ultimate objective cannot be accomplished with nuclear weapons, and that ground troops are required. These considerations are true for both limited and global warfare.

The Soviets, then, had recognized by the mid-1960s that non-nuclear operations at the unit and subunit levels would be an important component of any conflict, be it nuclear or non-nuclear. Therefore, discussions concerning these types of operations, particularly in tactical-level journals such as *Voyennyy Vestnik,* should not automatically be construed—as they often are—as evidence of Soviet interest in conducting only or primarily non-nuclear war. Even though *Voyennyy Vestnik* was designated the "combined-arms" journal in 1960, its focus was clearly directed to the subunit level.[20] Only rarely are unit level operations discussed, and operations of large units or formations are almost never treated. Thus, the articles deal almost exclusively with platoons, companies, and battalions; and reference to the non-nuclear character of these operations should not necessarily be interpreted to mean that the *overall conflict* is conventional.

Non-Nuclear War

The third factor is the Soviet interest in developing the capabilities for conducting non-nuclear war itself. In interpreting this interest, it is important to review the principal way in which the *Soviets* characterize war—i.e., according to its socio-political character. Among the major types of wars are those against counter-revolutionary movements (as witnessed in Hungary in 1956 and Czechoslovakia in 1968, and which might, in the future, occur in Poland or Yugoslavia), and wars of national revolution or liberation (e.g., in Afghanistan). Areas where Soviet forces might be needed in the future for this latter type of conflict

---

20. Even the "unit" or regiment should not yet be considered a combined-arms element.

include countries in the Middle East and, perhaps, selected European NATO countries. The Soviets prefer that both of these types of war should be carried out with non-nuclear capabilities. These *non-nuclear wars* thus pose a significant contrast to the probable character of war between the Warsaw Pact and NATO, which is viewed by both the Soviet Union and the West as likely to become nuclear (if it does not begin with nuclear weapons). As mentioned above, the primary conventional tasks are seen to occur possibly at the beginning and at the end of a Warsaw Pact-NATO war; they do not constitute the entire war.

Summary Statement of the Soviet Interest in Conventional Capabilities

The components of the Soviet interest in conventional capabilities were summarized in the 1969 edition of *Methodological Problems in Military Theory and Practice* as follows:

> All these [conventional] means preserve their value because of a number of reasons. In the first place wars without the utilization of nuclear weapons are possible. In the second place, if nuclear weapons will be used, then with their help it is not possible to solve all problems of armed combat, one cannot, for example, occupy the enemy's territory. Thirdly, on some objectives the utilization of nuclear weapons can be simply inadvisable. One must take into account that the utilization of a nuclear weapon under certain circumstances can interfere with the actions of our own troops. Finally, many conventional forms of weapons can be used very effectively for the annihilation of nuclear means of the enemy.[21]

While these interests were developing and being reflected in the Soviet literature, force posture, and training, there appeared a careful qualification by Colonel V.M. Bondarenko cautioning the military reader not to misinterpret the dialogue on conventional means as suggesting that nuclear war had declined in importance, or that the revolution in military affairs establishing the primacy of nuclear weapons had been reversed. On the contrary, he stressed, the develop-

---

21. A.S. Zheltove, et al., *Methodological Problems in Military Theory and Practice* (Moscow: 1969), FTD-MT-24-87-71, December 18, 1971, AD 738 734, p. 405.

ments leading toward the ability to operate in a non-nuclear fashion should be regarded as mere extensions of the basic revolution that was, and still is, nuclear.

The second circumstance [errors in understanding the "revolution in military affairs"] is a more serious one. It is involved with the fact that in our times conditions may arise when in individual instances combat operations may be carried out using conventional weapons. Under these conditions, the role of conventional means and the traditional services of armed forces are greatly increased. It becomes necessary to train troops for various kinds of warfare. This circumstance is sometimes interpreted as a negation of the contemporary revolution in military affairs as its conclusion.

One cannot agree with this opinion. The point is that the new possibilities of waging armed struggle have arisen not in spite of, but because of the nuclear missile weapons. They do not diminish their combat effectiveness, and the main thing, they do not preclude the possible use of such weapons. All this forces the conclusion that the present situation is one of the moments in the revolution in military affairs. It flows out of this revolution, continuing it, instead of contradicting it.

On the basis of this, we are able to define the contemporary revolution in military affairs as a radical upheaval in its development, which is characterized by new capabilities of attaining political goals in war, resulting from the availability of nuclear missile weapons to the troops.[22]

The nuclear weapon, new and massive, is seen as having triggered the "revolution." To carry the new weapon to its targets, revolutionary improvements in delivery systems (i.e., advances in missile and guidance technology) were developed. However, the revolution also brought increases in the conventional and traditional roles played by the military forces. In the Soviet view, there is no contradiction here; the increased roles for other military forces are seen as resulting from the advent of nuclear weapons.

---

22. V.M. Bondarenko, "The Modern Revolution in Military Affairs and the Combat Readiness of the Armed Forces," *Kommunist Vooruzhennykh Sil* [Communist of the Armed Forces], No. 24, edited and translated by Harriet Fast Scott, January 20, 1969, p. 8.

III. Advantages of Beginning a War with a Conventional Phase

The fourth and most interesting Soviet rationale for a conventional phase began to appear in Soviet doctrinal literature in the late 1960s and has continued to be set forth in writings throughout the 1970s. Western perceptions of the Soviet interest in conventional conflict have neglected this rationale. The basic idea behind this factor is that an inherent difficulty exists in launching a major offensive with a mass simultaneous nuclear strike. The following quote from *The Offensive,* for example, describes this difficulty:

> The simultaneous launching of nuclear strikes throughout the entire depth of the enemy's disposition is possible only with the presence of the corresponding quantity of nuclear ammunition and means for its delivery to the target as well as complete and reliable data on the enemy objectives throughout the entire depth of his defense. But the attacker will not always have such capabilities and data. It is considered difficult to determine the location of all objectives reliably and accurately for the launching of a simultaneous nuclear strike against them even with the presence of modern means of reconnaissance. And before destroying such objectives, final reconnaissance is required to refine their location. A portion of the objectives may be in motion or appear anew. Hence, the conclusion is drawn that one can hardly count on the fact that the attacker will succeed in destroying all important objectives with one simultaneous nuclear strike.[23]

The author, A.A. Sidorenko, is saying that it is not easy—and indeed may be impossible—to begin a war with a massive and decisive simultaneous nuclear strike. Numerous problems arise in the initiation of an

---

23. A.A. Sidorenko, *The Offensive* (A Soviet View) (Moscow: 1970), translated and published under the auspices of the U.S. Air Force, Soviet Military Thought Series No. 9 (Washington, D.C.: U.S. Government Printing Office, 1976), p. 114.

effective nuclear offense; key among them are the possibilities that the targets may not be identified or localized, and the weapon systems may not be ready. It is these problems which are believed to have led to the conclusion, as expressed in Soviet military writings, that considerable advantages reside in beginning a war with a conventional phase. The point of view taken in the Soviet and Warsaw Pact military literature explicitly emphasizes the opinion that such advantages would enable the Soviets to initiate offensive nuclear operations more effectively.

The first advantage the conventional phase provides is the opportunity to mobilize and deploy forces and shift the economy to a wartime basis. Not all Soviet forces are combat-ready; indeed, some may not even be deployed. Further, the Soviet economy, while extremely different from the economies of the Western countries, nevertheless is not fully geared to war status during peacetime; certain changes are required to bring it to a wartime state of readiness. The conventional phase is seen as providing the opportunity to initiate such actions.[24] For example, as stated in *Voyennaya mysl'* in 1967:

> . . . if military actions begin and in the course of a period of time are conducted without the use of nuclear weapons, then the country and the armed forces will have a certain minimum of time for mobilization and deployment of armed forces as well as for transferring the country's economy to a wartime system.[25]

Additionally:

> . . . the variant is not excluded whereby military operations will begin and will be conducted for some time with the use of merely conventional means of armed conflict. In this case the army, the state, and its economy will have some time to complete the strategic deployment of the armed forces, to take

---

24. The main beneficiary here might be the second strategic echelon, which is only partially manned and equipped in its day-to-day posture and which requires one to three days, depending on the unit deployment locations and missions, to become fully mobilized and combat-ready. (Interviews with a former East European senior officer, October–December, 1978.)

25. Col. Gen. M. Povaliy, "Development of Soviet Military Strategy," *Voyennaya mysl'*, No. 2, February 1967, FPD 0018/68, January 9, 1968, p. 71.

measures in mobilizing and concentrating the troops in theaters of military operations, and also to reorganize industry on a military footing.[26]

The availability and readiness of nuclear strike forces is a factor closely related to this mobilization. Apparently, many of these forces may not be in the theater, and those that are may not always be deployed in their wartime positions. A conventional phase provides the opportunity to move in and deploy these forces, and to bring them to the advanced stages of readiness that are required to execute a massive, simultaneous nuclear strike.

Such a beginning of war can create favorable conditions for the movement of all nuclear forces to the regions of combat operations, bringing them to the highest level of combat readiness, and subsequently inflicting the first nuclear strike with the employment in it of a maximum number of missile-launch sites, submarines, and aircraft at the most favorable moment.[27]

For both mobilization and readiness, the benefits of a conventional phase offer an additional dimension of particular importance. The actions concerning nuclear strike forces identified above, if detected, would serve to warn NATO, thus detracting from the element of surprise and, in this sense, operating to the disadvantage of the Soviet Union. As is consistently stressed in the Soviet literature, surprise carries the same significance today as it did during the late 1950s and early 1960s when the principles of nuclear conflict were originally being formulated: surprise in executing a nuclear strike is considered one of the most important conditions for success, and this applies whether the surprise nuclear attack is utilized to begin the war or as a means of transitioning to nuclear operations. In the Soviet view, the conventional phase permits preparatory actions to be carried out under the cover of conventional

---

26. Mar. SU N. Krylov, "The Nuclear Missile Shield of the Soviet State," *Voyennaya mysl'*, No. 11, November 1967, FPD 0157/68, November 18, 1968, pp. 17–18.
27. Maj. Gen. N. Vasendin and Col. N. Kuznetsov, "Modern Warfare and Surprise Attack," *Voyennaya mysl'*, No. 6, June 1968, FPD 005/69, January 16, 1969, p. 45.

combat operations, thus facilitating execution of the nuclear attack as a surprise attack. For example:

> . . . the movement of nuclear forces into regions of combat operations will be conducted in conditions of constant and active countermeasures of the defending side.
> . . . It is necessary to insure not only secrecy in bringing nuclear means to the regions of combat operations, but also constant protection of them from enemy strikes and secrecy and maximum speed in the preparation of the first strike.
> . . . The skillfully organized struggle against reconnaissance, the suppression of his radio-technical means, especially early detection systems, false and deceptive operations, and other measures can have a decisive influence on achievement of surprise in *switching to combat operations with the unlimited use of nuclear weapons.*[28]

The following excerpt from an article published in 1978 serves as a more recent example referring to the use of such covert preparations for execution of a surprise strike:

> Highly important principles have been developed in the course of Soviet strategy's development: constant readiness . . .; decisive massing . . .; covert preparations for and conduct of surprise strikes during repulsion of aggression; . . .[29]

A common way the Soviets describe the transition to nuclear operations is in terms of the notion of a surprise attack *during* a conflict.

Also closely related to readiness is survivability, as indicated in the quote above (reference 28). Of particular concern to the Soviets in this connection is the survivability of air and naval forces. The conventional phase provides the opportunity to disperse these forces (e.g., "completing the deployment of naval forces and posts for mobile basing"), thus increasing their survivability.[30]

---

28. *Ibid.* (Emphasis added.)
29. Col. Gen. F. Grayvoronskiy, "The Development of Soviet Operational Art," *Military Historical Journal*, No. 2, 1978, JPRS 70923, April 7, 1978, p. 46.
30. Maj. Gen. V. Zemskov, "Characteristic Features of Modern Wars and Possible Methods of Conducting Them," *Voyennaya mysl'*, No. 7, July 1969, FPD 0022/70, April 6, 1970, p. 23.

Advantages of Beginning a War with a Conventional Phase 21

Even though it is possible to argue that these advantages can be accrued to a certain extent through the holding of training and exercise maneuvers just prior to the beginning of the war, several of the more important advantages depend on the presence of war itself. A first example is related to the readiness of NATO forces and the implications for Soviet targeting of their expected dispersal on the eve of the war. As indicated in the earlier quotation from Sidorenko, the dispersal of NATO forces would mean the loss of targets. This loss in turn would render an *effective* simultaneous nuclear strike practically impossible. Thus, initiating the use of nuclear weapons under these conditions may not be sensible. A conventional phase would allow an opportunity to conduct massive reconnaissance to reacquire and identify targets for the nuclear strike. This reconnaissance can only be conducted during actual warfare, rather than during an exercise, because it is first and foremost an airborne operation requiring extensive overflight of NATO territory.

A second example is also associated with Soviet operations generally and reconnaissance in particular. Soviet doctrine places emphasis on the need for considerable operations behind-the-lines, carried out principally by airborne patrol and assault units inserted at the beginning of the war. These units play important roles in identifying NATO targets for nuclear strike, sabotaging NATO operations, and obtaining control of critical areas of terrain. However, their insertion takes time. A conventional phase would provide an opportunity to insert these units and allow them to become effective and operative prior to the nuclear strike. (It is particularly interesting to note the emphasis the Soviets place on nighttime operations for assault unit insertions.)

Third, the Soviets have concluded that conducting a nuclear strike without a rapidly following exploitation by ground and air forces is the wrong approach. The heart of the Soviet approach to war is the use of combined arms, which relies most importantly on the combination of nuclear strikes plus exploitation. As described by Lt. General V. Reznichenko, combined arms combat emphasizes actions by large units, units, and subunits of various arms and services coordinated in objectives, time, and place.[31] If these ground and air units are not prepared to exploit the nuclear strike, then the timing for that strike is not optimal.

---

31. Reznichenko, "Tactics—A Component Part of the Art of Warfare."

Such units cannot exploit a nuclear strike properly from their day-to-day postures; thus, the conventional phase is seen as providing the opportunity to get the first strategic echelon forces into a position from which the nuclear strike can be exploited.

Several factors are discussed in the Soviet literature that affect the positioning of forces during a conventional phase for purposes of exploitation, as described above. First, it is not clear what form the NATO defense will take—i.e., whether it will be positional, mobile, or some mixture of these. It is also not clear where the NATO forces will be. This is often described as a maldeployment problem from NATO's point of view; but, at the same time, it creates an uncertainty for the Soviets. The Soviets will not know in advance the extent to which the Western forces will have transitioned to wartime positions prior to the start of the war. A conventional phase will give the Soviet first echelon forces an opportunity to move in and through the NATO screening force or security zone, if one is established; to move into contact with the main NATO defense lines and identify strong points in the Western defense positions; and even to break through under certain conditions.

As described in *Voyennaya mysl'* in 1971, the existence of a security zone poses significant problems for the offensive. For example, it

> . . . makes it possible to place the main forces which are shifting to defense beyond the range of hostile tactical nuclear weapons, to conceal them from ground reconnaissance, ensures favorable conditions for requisite regrouping and effective employment of heavy construction equipment not only in defense depth but on the FEBA, and facilitates determination of the size of the attacking enemy force and the enemy's intentions before he reaches the main defensive positions.[32]

Until the Soviet forces have passed through the NATO screening force, they are not ready, in effect, to exploit a nuclear strike. Consider, for example, the following statement on the conventional phase:

> However, as has already been noted, the chief goal of operations of both sides in these conditions is considered to be the destruction in a short period

---

32. Col. G. Tonin and Col. K. Kushch-Zharko, "Defense in the Past and in the Present," *Voyennaya mysl'*, No. 7, July 1971, FPD 0014, March 7, 1974, p. 65.

Advantages of Beginning a War with a Conventional Phase 23

of the nuclear means, and above all those of operational-tactical designation, as well as a swift entry of the troops into operational depth and *insuring in the end maximum readiness for attack in conditions of the use of nuclear weapons.*[33]

Also, until the strong positions in the NATO main defense line have been identified, these positions are not targets for nuclear destruction.

Another factor is the Soviet concern over NATO atomic demolition munitions, which are seen as constituting a serious obstacle to an attacking force, as fallout creates severe problems for ground force operations. Delays of several hours and even days can result; one simply does not go through a fallout area without understanding the consequences of that movement. As has been pointed out in *Voyennaya mysl'*, "such a security zone, particularly if it contains nuclear land mines, will constitute a serious obstacle to an attacking force."[34] A conventional phase would provide the Soviets with the opportunity to move through those areas where NATO use of atomic demolition munitions is expected; to secure those areas; and, indeed, to destroy or capture the munitions that may have been emplaced.

For all these and perhaps other significant reasons, the Warsaw Pact forces have considerable reason to prefer transitioning to the use of nuclear weapons during, rather than at the start of, the war.

---

33. Col. D. Samorukov, "Combat Operations Involving Conventional Means of Destruction," *Voyennaya mysl'*, No. 8, August 1967, FPD 0125/68, April 26, 1968, p. 34. (Emphasis added.)

34. Tonin and Kushch-Zharko, "Defense in the Past and in the Present," p. 54.

IV. Characteristics of a Conventional Phase

A Conventional Phase "Under Threat of Nuclear Use"

In examining the Soviet approach to conventional conflict, it is important to recognize and keep always in mind that such conflict is considered one way in which a war between East and West can *begin;* that is, a war can contain an initial conventional or non-nuclear *phase.* The conventional conflict is not viewed as constituting the entire war, nor even as the likely way warfare will begin.[35]

As indicated earlier in this monograph, the Soviets expect a war which begins conventionally to go nuclear. In observing NATO, the Soviets see a threat that is nuclear-capable, has a strategy calling for the use of nuclear weapons in its defense, and regularly exercises the use of nuclear weapons in its war games and training. The Soviets also believe that the decisive portion of the war—and, hence, the most important part to prepare for—is the nuclear phase. As a consequence, the Soviet approach to a conventional phase stresses the related nuclear considerations and appears to be designed with transition to nuclear operations as the first and most dominant consideration. As stated in *Voyennaya mysl'* in 1968:

> . . . when selecting the method to be used in repelling an enemy's offensive, it is our opinion that initial consideration should be given to the use of nuclear weapons.[36]

---

35. This point is worth examining in greater detail, because the major tenet of U.S. policy has been to emphasize preparations (posture and plans) for what is regarded to be the most likely contingency (i.e., conventional) rather than the worst contingency (i.e., nuclear).

36. Col. L. Solov'yev and Col. S. Taran, "The Employment of Defense by the Ground Forces under Modern Conditions," *Voyennaya mysl'*, No. 12, December 1968, FPD 0102/69, November 3, 1969, p. 48.

A 1973 Soviet document reiterated this point:

> The *most important features*, which to a considerable degree will determine the composition of forces and materiel, and also the order of their use in intensification of troop efforts in an offensive, will be *the constant readiness to use nuclear weapons.*[37]

The Soviet approach to the conventional phase clearly reflects the fact that the focus of attention is on the nuclear war that is expected imminently; the conventional phase is to be designed so that the war can transition to nuclear weapons at a moment's notice. As a result, in the Soviet view a conventional phase would be fought in a manner quite different from the sort of war which might be extrapolated from World War II concepts. This suggests what may, in effect, represent a significant difference between the Soviet and Western approaches to conventional war planning.

Western planning for the conventional phase reflects what has been referred to as the dual capability dilemma. The problem, in NATO's view, centers on how to posture to fight both a conventional and a nuclear war when the two "require" dissimilar approaches. The dual capability dilemma, to NATO's way of thinking, flows from the basic inconsistency between the force concentration needed for conventional war and the dispersed posture required for nuclear conflict. On the other hand, the Soviet approach—i.e., to posture for the possibility that the war will suddenly go nuclear—causes them to address a somewhat different problem. In the Soviet view, it is no more permissible to concentrate forces in a war that might go nuclear than in a war that is already nuclear. Thus, the challenge for the Soviets primarily has been one of learning how to fight the conventional phase from a nuclear posture; hence, Soviet discussions of operations designed for the conventional phase sound very similar to their discussions of operations for a nuclear war. It is this factor which makes the problem of interpreting "non-nuclear" discussions, such as those most often encountered in *Voyennyy Vestnik*, extremely difficult.

---

37. Col. D. Samorukov, "Concerning the Intensification of Troop Efforts in an Offensive," *Voyennaya mysl'*, No. 10, October 1973, FPD 0063, November 21, 1974, p. 49. (Emphasis in original.)

Characteristics of a Conventional Phase

Numerous Soviet statements concerning the conventional phase indicate the similarities in structure and planning to nuclear warfighting. Regarding concentration or massing for attack, for example, one article says that

> . . . the massing of men and equipment on major axes will constitute a complex problem in operations conducted in a modern war. It will not be the same as in the last war, for the threat of enemy nuclear strike at any moment will make it necessary to effect concentration of troops with this threat taken into account.[38]

Thus, the conflict

> . . . between concentration and dispersal of forces is resolved by increasing force mobility, extensive utilization of military transport aircraft, helicopters, cross-country vehicles, etc. New means of displacement enable troops to effect rapid regroupings both parallel and perpendicular to the front under difficult conditions of terrain and weather, at considerable distances from bases of supply.[39]

Concentration becomes a question of timing and mobility—i.e., bringing together the required mass only briefly, breaking through or overcoming the defense, and then rapidly dispersing. This approach holds regardless of whether or not nuclear weapons have been used.

The operational structure also is similar for both types of conflict. For example, note the following excerpt from a 1966 issue of *Voyennaya mysl'*:

> During the threat of nuclear attack, the operational structure of defense and

---

38. General-Major A.S. Milovidov, editor-in-chief, *The Philosophical Heritage of V.I. Lenin and Problems of Contemporary War* (A Soviet View). This book was awarded the Frunze Prize in 1973, listed as recommended reading in "The Soldier's Bookshelf" section of the Soldier's Calendar for 1974, and still referenced as a most important text as recently as 1978. Translated and published under the auspices of the U.S. Air Force, Soviet Military Thought Series No. 5 (Washington, D.C.: U.S. Government Printing Office, 1974), p. 105.
39. *Ibid.*

advancing troops will be preserved in almost the same form we see for nuclear war conditions.[40]

The next year, an article stated:

> The following very important characteristic consists in the fact that to carry out the prescribed missions, both sides will need mainly the same forces which are indicated for the conduct of operations with the use of nuclear weapons. The fact is that the additional deployment of large forces for the beginning of an operation and, all the more, their concentration in certain zones or sectors of the front most likely cannot be used as a constant threat of use of nuclear weapons. Moreover, both sides will have to limit the use of these forces, keeping in mind the necessity of insuring constant readiness of a certain portion of their means for the use of nuclear weapons. This considerably decreases their combat capabilities, especially in the use of rocket troops and aviation.[41]

The direction of the attack also is planned with nuclear use foremost in mind. For example, as stated in *The Offensive* in 1970:

> . . . choosing the axis of main attack in such a way that nuclear weapons could be used most expediently . . . [to] take advantage of its results with greatest effect along with the high maneuver capabilities of *podrazdeleniya* for moving along the shortest routes to designated regions and complete the enemy rout in a short time.
>
> In choosing the axis of main attack, thorough consideration is made of the nature of the terrain and its possible change after nuclear strikes. Preference is given to those axes on which the terrain permits the employment of all combat arms, and above all tanks, and ensures the maximum use of maneuver capabilities of *podrazdeleniya*, concealed concentration and deployment of troops for an attack, and their swift advance into the depth right after nuclear strikes.[42]

---

40. Lt. Gen. (Res) B. Arushanyan, "Combat Operations by Tank Units Against Operational Defense Resources," *Voyennaya mysl'*, No. 1, January 1966, FDD 966, August 23, 1966, p. 34.
41. Samorvkov, "Combat Operrations Involving Conventional Means of Destruction," p. 31.
42. Sidorenko, *The Offensive*, p. 89.

Characteristics of a Conventional Phase

In 1973, the notion of conventional and nuclear similarities was addressed in *Voyennaya mysl'* from the point of view of defense:

> As regards the reinforcement and configuration of the defending troops, both in a nuclear war and under conditions of nonnuclear operations they will not be fundamentally different. Defense will always be of a dispersed and perimeter nature, while the defensive fire system should be based on the potential employment of nuclear weapons.[43]

Furthermore, the approach to mission assignment and the role of forward detachments reads almost identically for the conventional phase and for nuclear war. The following statement serves as an example:

> . . . attack from the march is considered the main method of offensive troop operations when nuclear weapons are employed. But will this be the main method of troop operations when nuclear weapons are not employed? If discussing an attack against an enemy who has hastily assumed the defense, the answer to this question is affirmative.[44]

As in the nuclear case, the individual units during the conventional phase are not to get bogged down fighting NATO units, but are to proceed rapidly into the enemy's rear.

> Large units of the first echelon carrying out the encirclement and destruction will boldly and daringly penetrate through gaps and holes deep into the enemy operational formations, split and quickly crush isolated enemy troops unit by unit, and destroy nuclear weapons, reserves, and control points. For the most rapid completion of the rout, it is necessary that strikes for the purpose of splitting and destroying encircled enemy groupings be delivered even as early as during the process of encirclement maneuvers, not waiting until basic routes of withdrawal are seized.[45]

---

43. Col. I. Andreyevich, "Problems of Modern Defense," *Voyennaya mysl'*, No. 6, June 1973, FPD 0031, June 5, 1974, p. 87.

44. Cols. M. Fedulov, M. Shmelev, A. Sinyayev, and I. Lyutov, "Problems of Modern Combined-Arms Combat," *Voyennaya mysl'*, No. 10, October 1964, FDD 914, May 30, 1965, p. 29.

45. Maj. Gen. G. Kuvlanov, "Airborne Landings and the Struggle Against Them," *Voyennaya mysl'*, No. 8, August 1965, FDD 958, April 22, 1966, p. 57.

Along these same lines:

> It is advantageous that attacks for the purposes of splintering the enemy be delivered in the shortest directions and in those sectors where the enemy cannot use previously prepared lines and where he does not have strong reserves.[46]

Soviet statements such as these indicate the existence of strong similarities between nuclear and conventional tactics. Statements can also be found which reveal similarities between nuclear and conventional conflict with respect to the role of surprise, the chief goals and selection of missions, and even chosen targets. The main differences between a nuclear conflict and a conflict conducted under the threat of going nuclear are found in the approaches to meeting engagements and in the roles of artillery and air power, which in the conventional phase would necessarily cover tasks that in a nuclear conflict would be handled by nuclear missiles.

The following is a typical statement illustrating the role of air power in a conventional phase:

> The use of air power is somewhat different in those areas where military operations will employ only conventional weapons. If the ground forces launch the main attack primarily against a weak spot in the enemy's operational formation air power must be brought to bear not only against the enemy force in that area but also against enemy nuclear weapon-carrying aircraft and missiles. Neutralization of enemy nuclear weapon-carrying aircraft and missiles will constitute the major task, which will require a large number of aircraft. Therefore only limited air power can be assigned to support ground operations. The requisite degree of massed air power employment in the area of the main ground force thrust is achieved primarily by reducing the width and depth of combat operations. This in turn conditions the character of the process of overwhelming the opposing ground force, based on sequential thrusts aimed at deep penetration.[47]

---

46. Maj. Gen. S. Shtrik, "The Encirclement and Destruction of the Enemy During Combat Operations Not Involving the Use of Nuclear Weapons," *Voyennaya mysl'*, No. 1, January 1968, FPD 0093/68, May 22, 1968, p. 57.

47. Col. Yu. Bryuklanov, "The Massed Employment of Aircraft," *Voyennaya mysl'*, No. 6, June 1969, FPD 0008/70, January 30, 1970, p. 45.

With respect to artillery:

> Artillery will play a quite different role in conducting defensive operations with the use of just conventional means of conflict. In these conditions, artillery, as the chief means of destruction, must be ready at the necessary moment to drop on the attacker the entire might of its fire. Before and at the beginning of an attack, it must inflict jointly with aircraft the maximum losses against the enemy with concentrated and mass fire, disrupt his combat formations, and force him to stop any further attack. Also, with the approach of the enemy to the forward edge of defense, artillery must block his path with barrage fire and destroy with direct laying of fire the troops which have penetrated the barrage fire.[48]

In both cases, the problems posed by these different roles have probably been mitigated by the growth that has taken place since the article cited above was written in ground-attack tactical air forces and in artillery, both towed and self-propelled. Significant additional differences in several areas do exist, however, depending upon whether the war starts with a nuclear strike or with a conventional phase; this is especially true in the scheduling of certain operations such as air reconnaissance and airborne assault, in nuclear targeting, and in coordinating strikes with the maneuver of exploiting units. These differences, however, are command and control issues principally under the purview of the Front and General Staff. The main problem for the Soviets appears to be the following: if the war starts conventionally and involves massive air reconnaissance and airborne assault unit insertion, it might be difficult to transition to nuclear operations when those activities are under way.

Characteristic Features of a Conventional Phase

As described by the editor of *Voyennaya mysl'* in 1969, the most important features of non-nuclear operations are:

- Concentration of the main forces for destruction—above all, the means of nuclear attack—at their bases and regions of deployment

---

48. Col. P. Shkarubskiy, "The Artillery in Modern Combat Operations of the Ground Forces," *Voyennaya mysl'*, No. 6, June 1968, FPD 0005/69, January 16, 1969, p. 64.

- Retaining in constant readiness the strategic and operational-tactical nuclear means of operations
- Regular elaboration of plans for their combat use in accordance with the changing situation
- Constant and fast reinforcement of groupings of troops in the main zones by moving forward the reserves from the depths of the countries of the coalitions
- Completing the deployment of naval forces and posts for mobile basings
- Echeloning and utilizing the forces and means in connection with allocating the forces, mainly aircraft, of the so-called "nuclear echelons"[49]

These features can be divided into two major subsets: those that involve the focus of the conventional effort and those that involve readiness to transition to nuclear warfare.

The focus of the conventional effort is to counter NATO nuclear forces and to place Warsaw Pact forces in the position most advantageous for exploitation of the nuclear strike. As elaborated in *Voyennaya mysl'* in 1967, during the conventional phase one must:

. . . concentrate forces for a strike only against the most important objectives.

. . . decrease to the maximum the number of forces and means for carrying out a number of other missions, especially those whose fulfillment requires considerable time and the achieved result of which does not directly influence a great decrease in the nuclear capabilities of the enemy.

. . . [pursue as] the chief goal of operations . . . the destruction in a short period of the nuclear means, and above all those of operational-tactical designation, as well as a swift entry of the troops into operational depth and insuring in the end maximum readiness for attack in conditions of the use of nuclear weapons.[50]

The concern with the readiness to transition is seen most clearly in the emphasis on readiness of the nuclear strike forces, the scheduling of

---

49. Zemskov, "Characteristic Features of Modern Wars and Possible Methods of Conducting Them," p. 23.

50. Samorukov, "Combat Operations Involving Conventional Means of Destruction," p. 31.

Characteristics of a Conventional Phase   33

missions for the assault forces, and the handling of the second echelon and reserve forces. Of first and critical importance is "retaining in constant readiness the strategic and operational-tactical nuclear means for operations" and the "regular elaboration of plans for their combat use in accordance with the changing situation"[51]:

> In conducting combat operations without the use of nuclear weapons, the rockets of the ground troops must be maintained in constant readiness since changes of the situation continuously make their tasks more specific, and change or redesignate the targets of attack. Appropriate correctives in planning are required in the event of a shift to nuclear operations.[52]

And:

> ... in the utilization of conventional means a portion of the aircraft ... will be in constant readiness to use nuclear weapons. ....[53]

Targets for nuclear strike are said to be updated on a routine weekly basis, prior to the start of the war. As the war becomes more imminent, updating shifts to a daily basis; and once the war starts, it occurs on what appears to be an hourly or possibly continuous basis.[54] All targets are

---

51. Zemskov, "Characteristic Features of Modern Wars and Possible Methods of Conducting Them," p. 23.
52. Shtrik, "The Encirclement and Destruction of the Enemy During Combat Operations Not Involving the Use of Nuclear Weapons," p. 60.
53. Col. N. Semenov, "Gaining Supremacy in the Air," *Voyennaya mysl'*, No. 4, April 1968, FPD 0052/69, May 27, 1969, p. 44.
54. On October 3, 1964, the heads of military intelligence from all the Warsaw Pact countries, with the exception of Rumania, met in Moscow. As a result of this meeting, it was decided to construct intelligence processing information centers in each Warsaw Pact country to collect and integrate intelligence information on NATO forces, and to supply this information to their respective general staffs. Over the years 1965–1967, this decision was implemented. For example, in Czechoslovakia a major center was built at Litomerice, which was fed by numerous other "satellite" collection stations. Here integration and analyses of mainly electronic intelligence emanating from Germany, Italy, and Greece were performed, and provided on an hourly basis to the Czech general staff. (Interviews with a former East European senior officer, October–December, 1978.)

assigned to nuclear forces during the conventional phase of the war. These targets are also attacked by non-nuclear forces during the non-nuclear phase; when a target has been destroyed, the nuclear system that was covering it is assigned a new target. Thus, all enemy points of importance to the Warsaw Pact are continuously targeted by the nuclear force, which is to be prepared for a mass strike at any time.

The second aspect of the readiness to transition concerns ground force mission assignment and planning. In planning each mission or other activity, the assumption that the war may go nuclear at any time is taken into account, and a basic nuclear annex is prepared for this contingency. The establishment of general missions and goals explicitly is considered unacceptable; instead, very specific missions and goals are identified, thus making easier the planning for transition at any particular moment. For example, as explained in *Voyennaya mysl'* in 1967:

> . . . it is required that at any moment the overall operation of the troops have a completed cycle, i.e., that a specific goal would be achieved, even a limited goal, but one which must be a part of the main goal and the troops would be ready to the maximum extent to carry out their assigned missions without the use of nuclear weapons and to operate in conditions of their use.[55]

The second echelon forces constitute a further aspect of transition readiness. The second echelon armies and the reserves are the forces that complete the victory, destroy the opponent's vestigial forces, and consolidate the gains achieved by the first echelon forces. A special problem addressed in the Soviet literature concerns the role of these forces in a conventional phase. The use assigned to them appears to differ somewhat from the role undertaken in previous wars. Because of the possibility that the war might go nuclear at any instant, force missions must be well planned and very specific. In addition, it is difficult to know in advance which direction of attack the second echelon should take, not to mention the problems involved in the allocation of specific missions. As stated in 1968:

> . . . in modern operations it will be extremely difficult to determine beforehand the specific missions for the second echelon.[56]

---

55. Povaliy, "Development of Soviet Military Strategy," p. 40.
56. "The 150th Birthday of Karl Marx the Founder of Scientific Communism," *Voyennaya mysl'*, No. 5, May 1968, FPD 0013/69, February 4, 1969, p. 4.

Characteristics of a Conventional Phase

Also, because these forces require great mobility and would be lucrative nuclear targets for the enemy, there is additional concern for their safety should their location and presence be revealed to NATO.

Moreover, we cannot but consider that the troops which are being transferred even at great distances from the front are outside their shelters and therefore constitute favorable targets for nuclear strikes of the enemy. This, in turn, limits the possibility of maneuver by second echelons and reserves.[57]

Therefore, the Soviets stress the need during the initial conventional phase to conceal and maneuver the second echelon forces so as to avoid giving away their position. Rather than making these forces immediately available to support the first echelon forces, the Soviets discuss the possibility of holding them back during the conventional phase, thus insuring their availability to move out and exploit the nuclear strike when and if it comes. Consider, for example, the following passage from *The Offensive:*

> A deeply echeloned combat formation also favors the conduct of flexible maneuver in the course of combat, inasmuch as maneuver from the depth is more advantageous and simpler to accomplish *in the course of an attack*. The commitment of second echelons and reserves permits a rapid shift of efforts to new axes and maneuver for the purpose of delivering a blow at the enemy's flank and rear, making rapid use of *results of nuclear strikes in the course of combat,* repulsing enemy counterattacks, and replacing first echelon podrazdeleniya [small or subunits] which have lost combat effectiveness.[58]

The Soviets have remarked that in a conventional phase "most often there will be no second echelon in such a form as a field army."[59]

In *Voyennaya mysl'* in 1973 the Soviets reviewed in a broader discussion the role of the second echelon:

> In modern operations, just as during the years of World War II, the second echelons are to be used for developing the success on the main axes.

---

57. Maj. Gen. S. Begunov, "The Maneuver of Forces and Material in an Offensive," *Voyennaya mysl'*, No. 5, May 1968, FPD 0013/69, February 4, 1969, p. 45.
58. Sidorenko, *The Offensive,* p. 91. (Emphasis added.)
59. Povaliy, "Development of Soviet Military Strategy," p. 38.

Moreover, in the opinion of western military specialists they can be used for repelling counter attacks and counter thrusts by the enemy, and for defeating his counter thrust groupings. In a favorable situation they can be used for developing the success toward the flank for the purpose of encircling and destroying the main enemy grouping. Also not excluded is the possibility of using the second echelons for destroying enemy groupings and centers of resistance which remain in the rear of the advancing side. A new mission which the second echelons did not have to carry out previously is the reinforcing or replacing of first echelon troops which suffer great losses from nuclear strikes.

At the same time certain tasks which during the years of the Great Patriotic War often fell to the second echelons most probably will not arise under modern conditions. One of them could be the participation of the second echelons in carrying out the breakthrough of the tactical defensive zone. At present the tank and mechanized combined units are armed with a large number of tanks, armored personnel carriers and other armored vehicles. As a result they are able to create the tactical densities which will make it possible to pierce the enemy defenses to the entire tactical depth at high tempos and without committing additional forces.[60]

In sum, the characteristic features of a conventional phase, as presented in the Soviet literature, seem to be dominated by the nuclear war that is expected to follow. That nuclear war is considered the decisive event, and the conventional phase is used primarily in preparation for it.

Specific Tasks

As indicated in several of the foregoing quotations, the chief goals of the initial conventional phase are the destruction of the enemy's nuclear means and the swift entry of troops into the operational depth. The combined objective of these goals is to facilitate the transition to nuclear weapons—i.e., to prepare for the strike plus exploitation. The major individual tasks are almost self-evident.

Consider first the goal of destroying NATO's nuclear means. The most obvious task is mounting direct attacks on the loci of NATO's nuclear capabilities—i.e., known air bases, missile units, and storage sites. A second task is destroying the associated Command, Control,

---

60. Col. A. Poltavets, "Use of Support Echelons and Reserves in Offensive Operations," *Voyennaya mysl'*, No. 8, August 1973, FPD 0038, July 10, 1974.

Characteristics of a Conventional Phase 37

Communications, and Intelligence (C^3I). The command, control and target acquisition systems are considered by the Soviets as part of NATO's nuclear means; and in several respects, the Soviets view such ancillary systems as the most important part.

> In order to make it difficult for the enemy to use nuclear weapons, it is also necessary to combat actively and destroy the links which directly support the infliction of nuclear strikes (storage areas of nuclear weapons, control posts, and reconnaissance organs).
>
> In other words, a well-organized system of combat is needed which permits the reliable destruction of both the carriers of nuclear weapons and the forces and means which support them.[61]

The third task is to gain air superiority, so as to enable reconnaissance flights, facilitate the insertion of airborne assault units, and debilitate NATO nuclear air capability. This task has three sub-tasks: the attack on NATO fighter airbases; the destruction of associated C^3I (e.g., Ground Control Intercept [GCI] radars and navigation electronics); and the neutralization of NATO air defenses, which in fact is principally an attack on C^3I (in particular, the acquisition radars). The fourth important task is the insertion of airborne assault units both to reconnoiter and to sabotage NATO nuclear capabilities.

In noting the importance of NATO nuclear aviation, the Soviets have observed that 70 to 80 percent of all nuclear weapons in NATO exercises are delivered by tactical aviation. Therefore, the Soviets direct substantial effort toward winning air superiority immediately at the start of the war. This is not just a task for frontal aviation; rather, as in the accomplishment of other tasks, all forces and means are employed, including strategic aviation, ground forces, naval forces, airborne assault forces, and special Electronic Warfare units.

> In organizing the battle for air superiority the main idea is invariably retained as before, i.e., the need for joint effort by different branches of the armed forces to accomplish the problem in question.[62]

---

61. Shkarubskiy, "The Artillery in Modern Combat Operations of the Ground Forces," p. 66.
62. Col. F. Shesterin, "The Experience of the Battle for Air Superiority in World War II and Its Significance Under Modern Conditions," *Voyennaya mysl'*, No. 2, February 1969, FPD 0060/69, June 18, 1969, p. 72.

The second goal—the rapid placement of troops in the operational depth—can also be divided into several major tasks. First, airborne assault forces must be inserted to seize critical areas of terrain for purposes of facilitating movement of the main Soviet forces when they arrive and forestalling NATO mobilization and force movements. Performance of this task would be reliant on the previously discussed task of gaining air superiority. The second major task is undertaking the main assault with the first echelon ground forces. The basic concept underlying the combined-arms assault would be the rapid movement of advanced detachments into the NATO rear, as in the nuclear variant. For example, with reference to the conventional variant:

> . . . strong and maneuverable advanced detachments which have a high degree of independence are very broadly used in the combat structure of formations in large units of attacking troops in order to carry out very quickly many important missions . . . such as the destruction or seizing of enemy missile units and guidance and control posts.[63]

The purpose of the mission is to get into NATO's rear, not to attack the main defense positions head-on. The forces are to avoid major force engagements whenever possible, leaving the destruction of enemy forces to the nuclear strike that follows. If the latter does not materialize, the destruction of enemy forces will be handled by the ground-attack air and second echelon forces as part of their job of developing the breakthroughs achieved by the first echelon. The third task under this goal is to gain air superiority in order to protect the advance detachments from NATO ground-attack tactical air power, and to enable Warsaw Pact ground-attack air to provide both reconnaissance support and fire support as the detachments outrun their organic artillery fire support. The fourth task is to seize NATO airbases, both military and non-military, for use by Pact Frontal Aviation in providing the support identified above and by Soviet transport aviation (LRA) in accomplishing large-scale, air-mobile force landings in NATO's depth. Destruction of NATO C^3I is an important component objective of all these tasks, just as it was in the case of attacking NATO's nuclear means.

A third goal, not mentioned above because it is primarily a political-

---

63. Samorukov, "Combat Operations Involving Conventional Means of Destruction," p. 39.

strategic goal, is to seize important political-administrative, industrial, and economic targets, both for Soviet use and to deny their availability to NATO (e.g., oil). For this goal, the primary task would be the mounting of airborne and seaborne assault operations against particular objectives.

When the above-described tasks are considered together, it can be seen that the paramount force operations required are:

- Attack on all NATO airbases—nuclear, reconnaissance, and tactical
- Attack on NATO air defenses
- Massive penetration by air reconnaissance, airborne assault, and landing operations
- Attack with high speed forward detachments
- Attack on NATO C^3I

The last operation in this list is particularly critical, in that it directly applies to almost every other major task—i.e., to the destruction of the enemy's nuclear means, the gaining of air superiority, the neutralization of air defenses, and the forestalling of NATO mobilization and force movements. Command and control are considered to be the most vulnerable aspects of the NATO systems; this is seen as applicable to NATO communications in all cases, to radars in the case of air defense, and to the ground control intercept radars and navigation means in the case of the battle for air superiority.

> The most important prerequisite for successful solution to the problem of struggle for air superiority under present conditions is absolute suppression of the enemy's means of control including the means of controlling aviation and the PVO system.[64]

To the Soviets, the battle against command and control includes as targets

> . . . the organs and points of control computer centers and communications warning and information systems. Early detection and warning and also

---

64. Shesterin, "The Experience of the Battle for Air Superiority in World War II and Its Significance Under Modern Conditions," p. 74.

space and navigation tracking systems are directly connected with it and are essentially one of its component parts.[65]

This attack on NATO C³I clearly is not limited to an electronic warfare (EW) attack; EW comprises only one-sixth of the effort. Other means to be utilized in the attack include conventional air power, chemical munitions, ground-based firepower, advanced detachments of the ground forces, and airborne Army and seaborne Naval assault units.

To disorganize the control systems of the aircraft (including the navigation systems) and the air-defense means, the combatants will strive to employ broadly and are employing (as is indicated by postwar events and conflicts) along with the aircraft the services of radiotechnical troops, airborne troops, naval forces, and diversionary and other detachments. Experience shows that detachments even consisting of several men which are landed from submarines or dropped from aircraft can destroy or put out of commission for a long time radar stations, control towers, long-range and short-range homing airport stations, glide-path and approach beacons, equipment for instrument landings, etc. All these operations are usually complemented broadly by false orders and misinformation capable of leading the flight personnel and crews of the control posts into error and leading to confusion and error of judgment.[66]

Finally, the use of numerous passive decoy and deception techniques to confuse both NATO target acquisition and signal intelligence capabilities also is integrated into the Soviet Radio Electronic Combat (REC) plan. Under the rubric of REC, the Soviets have consolidated the totality of their planned, tightly-integrated offensive against NATO C³I, using all forces and means.

---

65. Mar. SU V. Sokolovskiy and Maj. Gen. M. Cherednichenko, "Military Strategy and its Problems," *Voyennaya mysl'*, No. 10, October 1968, FPD 0084/69, August 29, 1969, p. 41.

66. Semenov, "Gaining Supremacy in the Air," p. 44.

V. Transition to Nuclear Operations

As indicated earlier in this monograph, the Soviets believe that the most important period of a war in Europe will be the nuclear portion. The initial mass nuclear strike is viewed as being able to determine the outcome of the war very quickly and suddenly. Soviet doctrine and its corresponding strategy call for a nuclear first strike in which surprise is a most important characteristic. Surprise plays a critical role in two respects: a) to catch the enemy unaware, thus maximizing the effectiveness of the Soviet strike; and b) to ensure at the same time that the Warsaw Pact forces are not surprised by a NATO nuclear strike. The main thrust of Soviet strategy can best be described as first-strike and offensive, and the Soviet approach to the problem of transitioning to nuclear operations can best be understood as one of seeking to identify "the most favorable time" to go nuclear.

Transitioning to nuclear operations is not a simple matter of merely launching a nuclear strike, however, because the safety of friendly units must be considered, along with their readiness to exploit the effects of the strike. For example, if the strike is to be made at night, the problem of flash blindness makes it imperative that extra care be taken to warn friendly forces, particularly those which are airborne. It might also be unwise to execute a strike during a time of considerable activity in the form of mass reconnaissance flights or insertion of behind-the-lines operations units. It also is necessary to locate and warn the forward units so that they have time to take cover, or at least to give them boundary lines that they are not to cross before a certain time.[67] Additional dispersal of units expected to be targeted by NATO might also be accomplished so as to increase their survivability and diminish the effectiveness of any NATO retaliation. Note the following excerpt from a 1968 issue of *Voyennaya mysl'*:

---

67. Joseph D. Douglass, Jr., *The Soviet Theater Nuclear Offensive*, Studies in Communist Affairs (Washington, D.C.: U.S. Government Printing Office, 1976), pp. 58–59.

The withdrawal of troops from under enemy nuclear strikes will also be used in a modern nuclear war. Such operations are frequently referred to in literature as antiatomic maneuver. Implied here mainly is a change of regions of disposition of troops and of position of regions of fire means for the purpose of retaining them from the effects of weapons of mass destruction of the enemy. This is achieved by the prompt transfer of forces and by occupying regions which insure their withdrawal from under possible enemy strikes or which provide the maximum degree of protection from the effects of nuclear weapons. The change in regions of disposition of troops is made periodically, quickly, and secretly. The previous conditions are maintained in the evacuated regions in a number of cases.[68]

The Soviets see their transportation net as constituting a particularly important target for NATO nuclear strikes. They speak therefore of the need to stop the transportation of all supplies and units when the exchange of nuclear strikes is expected to take place, and to separate such units from obvious transportation targets; the movement of these supplies and forces will be resumed along alternate paths following the major nuclear exchange. In summary, the Soviets—under the assumption that they will be able to control to a lesser or greater extent when the war goes nuclear—appear to have planned a variety of anti-atomic maneuvers in association with the transition to nuclear operations.

If at all possible, the Soviets clearly intend to be the first party to strike with nuclear weapons, thereby preempting any perceived NATO intention to mount a massive nuclear strike. Accordingly, the first priority for Soviet strategic intelligence is to detect any NATO decision to initiate nuclear operations, and the first priority for tactical intelligence is to detect any actions taken to carry out such a decision. Preemption is associated principally with a NATO mass use of nuclear weapons, not necessarily with a limited use of nuclear weapons. It is difficult to define what constitutes a "mass use" in terms of numbers of weapons, but anything over 100 would certainly be regarded as falling in this category.

In this connection, V. Ye. Savkin's *Basic Principles of Operational Art and Tactics,* published in 1972, contains a particularly interesting quote concerning numbers:

---

68. Begunov, "The Maneuver of Forces and Material in an Offensive," p. 45.

Transition to Nuclear Operations 43

The number of new means needed for a change of methods of combat operations is inversely proportional to their combat power. For machine guns this figure reached hundreds of thousands of units, and for tanks and aviation—several thousand. *The production of several hundred nuclear weapons and means of delivery at one time caused a need for fundamental revision* of methods and forms of combat operations. The number of nuclear weapons is constantly building up.[69]

One might infer two points from this quote: a) that the Soviet stockpile of nuclear weapons in the mid-1950s, when the nuclear revolution began, was several hundred in number; and b) that a modern war using nuclear weapons would involve at least several hundred of these weapons. The smallest number associated with a "mass" strike that has been identified in the Soviet literature is "scores" of weapons.[70] Therefore, it might not be unreasonable to postulate the following schedule:

Type of Strike	Numbers of Weapons
Individual	1
Group	Several to 20
Mass	50 or more

In the event of an extremely limited use of nuclear weapons by NATO, it is difficult to hypothesize precisely what the Soviet response would be. It does appear, however, that the Soviets do not have a high regard for the very limited use of nuclear weapons, since such a usage is viewed by definition as not contributing to changing the course of the war. Hence, if the Soviets were not in a favorable position for transitioning to nuclear operations at that time, a very limited use by NATO might well be ignored, or at least not produce an immediate reaction. Rather, the Soviet focus would be on undertaking all measures necessary to most effectively implement—with the greatest element of surprise—a mass nuclear strike at the soonest favorable time. It is also possible that the

---

69. V. Ye. Savkin, *Basic Principles of Operational Art and Tactics* (A Soviet View) (Moscow: 1972), translated and published under the auspices of the U.S. Air Force, Soviet Military Thought Series No. 9 (Washington, D.C.: U.S. Government Printing Office), p. 109. (Emphasis added.)

70. Maj. Gen. G. Biryukov and Col. G. Melnikov, *Antitank Warfare* (Moscow: Progress Publishers, 1972), p. 105.

Soviets might respond in a "limited" fashion to mislead NATO and buy time while their mass strike was under preparation.[71]

Because of the importance of striking first with maximum surprise and the need to undertake certain anti-nuclear maneuvers in the final pre-strike stage, the Soviets emphasize the need not only to watch for intelligence indicators but also to *anticipate* Western decisions and act before NATO does. Thus, considerable effort is expended on analyzing NATO strategy and assessing Western intentions through extensive analysis of NATO military literature and exercises. Unquestionably the Soviets face a severe challenge in interpreting what they read and see regarding NATO strategy. This strategy calls for the use of nuclear weapons either in response to utilization of such weapons by the Soviet Union, or to avoid the defeat of a significant segment of Western forces or the capture of a significant portion of NATO territory. As recognized in *Voyennaya mysl'* in 1969:

> . . . a nuclear attack with limited goals is specified by the NATO leadership as one of the variants of unleashing a war in the secondary theaters of military operations, but it is not excluded even in Europe. True, in the latter case it is hardly probable that military operations will succeed for any length of time in staying within a limited framework. Most likely they will grow into a general nuclear war. The most dangerous in this regard might be the periods when a crisis situation is created for the aggressor and there is imminent danger of destruction of his armed forces or loss of most important regions of territory in the theater of military operations, and therefore he switches to unlimited use of the entire arsenal of nuclear means.[72]

NATO initiation of use of nuclear weapons in a conventional phase appears to be associated most commonly with a successful Soviet breakthrough operation. As stated by the U.S. Secretary of Defense in 1977:

> . . . in structuring U.S. nuclear forces, attacks in Central Europe or in Korea are considered the most likely to call for backup. A decision to use tactical nuclear weapons would depend upon (1) an enemy conventional

---

71. Douglass, *The Soviet Theater Nuclear Offensive*, pp. 106–107.

72. Maj. Gen. V. Zemskov, "Wars of the Modern Era," *Voyennaya mysl'*, No. 5, May 1969, FPD 0117/69, December 18, 1969, p. 61.

Transition to Nuclear Operations

breakthrough which could not be countered, or (2) his first use of nuclear weapons.[73]

This basic approach is also supported by what the Soviets are able to observe in NATO exercises. Because a Soviet breakthrough could occur fairly early in the course of the war (and certainly in the first few days), and because the Soviets recognize the problems in the NATO coalition of reaching a decision to use nuclear weapons, the Soviet assessment of the NATO political process may also support the assumption that NATO would not be able to use nuclear weapons in advance of such a breakthrough.

However, the flood of stories associated with British and U.S. cover and deception during World War II, as well as the Soviet Union's own propensities in this vein, might well cause the Soviets to have second thoughts with respect to the above-mentioned assumption. To further understand this problem, it is necessary to recognize the difference between a) policy measures designed to prepare, initiate, and conduct war (action policy); and b) statements and actions that convey capability and intent, appropriately slanted so as to influence the actions of the opponent (declaratory policy). Both Soviet and U.S. leaders have recognized that striking first in modern warfare carries significant advantages in terms of the course and results of the war; therefore, a first strike objective might well be a component of the action policy of both sides. In support of this action policy, however, declaratory policy must portray a very different objective; otherwise, the situation would be gravely destabilized, since the enemy would be driven toward early preemption. With these considerations in mind, the declaratory policy of the United States should reflect internal confidence in the West's nuclear capability and in its ability to survive a first strike and retaliate, whether or not this constitutes an accurate portrayal of reality. It is logical to assume that the Soviets understand this dichotomy as well.

When to Strike

As indicated earlier, the Soviets do not intend to attempt to raise the nuclear threshold or extend the conventional phase as long as possible.

---

73. Donald H. Rumsfeld, Secretary of Defense, *Department of Defense Annual Report, Fiscal Year 1978,* January 17, 1977, p. 22.

Rather, they will seek to identify what is from their point of view "the most favorable moment,"[74] and will transition to nuclear warfare at that time. Consider, for example, the following passage from a 1969 *Voyennaya mysl'* article:

> In our time special importance is attached to the skill of commanders and staffs in the timely and accurate evaluation of the combat capabilities of friendly and enemy troops, and for ascertaining not only the quantitative, but also, which is especially important at the present time, the hidden and qualitative correlation of forces. It is important to use variants of models of a dynamic (current change) correlation of forces worked out in advance for the most typical military situations, using for this purpose modern methods of research operations, including mathematical. It is important for command personnel to be able to make strict account of actual conditions and in accordance with this to determine which factor at a given time is decisive for changing the balance of forces and achieving superiority over the enemy. It is important for them to be able to determine correctly imminent crisis moments of operations, to select the right time for committing to action supplementary and reserve forces and means on decisive axes for the purpose of creating that ratio of forces which will assure the attainment of a decisive success.[75]

Further, from Col. M. P. Skirdo's *The People, The Army, The Commander:*

> Most important in a military leader's foresight is his ability to detect the basic tendencies in the development of an armed struggle. This permits him to foretell with the required accuracy the moment when the correlation of forces should be changed.[76]

---

74. Vasendin and Kuznetsov, "Modern Warfare and Surprise Attack," p. 45.

75. Col. S. Tyushkevich, "The Methodology for the Correlation of Forces in War," *Voyennaya mysl'*, No. 6, June 1969, FPD 0008/70, January 30, 1970, p. 37.

76. Col. M.P. Skirdo, *The People, The Army, The Commander* (A Soviet View) (Moscow: 1970), translated and published under the auspices of the U.S. Air Force, Soviet Military Thought Series No. 14 (Washington, D.C.: U.S. Government Printing Office, 1978), p. 146.

Transition to Nuclear Operations

In trying to understand how "the most favorable moment" might be determined, four items of importance stand out. The first concerns the position of the first strategic echelon forces, which should be in position to exploit the nuclear strike. It seems, therefore, that the most favorable time would occur after these forces had penetrated NATO screening defenses and encountered the main line of Western defenses, either running into opposition or finding themselves on the verge of breaking through. When the attack forces are ready to break through, they are prepared to exploit the nuclear strike. When they have encountered opposition, they thereby are able to identify the major target areas for operational-tactical nuclear strikes in order to open a breech through which the forces can advance for exploitation purposes.

The second item concerns the status of the second strategic echelon forces, or those second echelon and reserve forces that are intended to develop the breakthrough produced by the first echelon. As a general rule, the first echelon forces are responsible for breaking through and getting into NATO's rear as fast as possible, as has been noted above. Wherever possible, they are to avoid any serious force confrontations, which would serve only to bog down the advance. It is the second echelon that is responsible for taking care of the remaining NATO forces and for developing or consolidating the breakthrough. When these second echelon forces move forward, they become vulnerable to NATO nuclear strikes; therefore, great importance is attached to the decision to commit them.

> Moreover, we cannot but consider that the troops which are being transferred even at great distances from the front are outside their shelters and therefore constitute favorable targets for nuclear strikes of the enemy. This in turn, limits the possibility of maneuver by second echelons and reserves.[77]

It is considered important not to commit these forces too early, because if the war does go nuclear, it is possible that the first echelon forces may suffer considerable damage, necessitating replacement of the latter by portions of the second echelon in exploiting the nuclear strikes. The decision to commit the second echelon forces often appears

---

77. Begunov, "The Maneuver of Forces and Material in an Offensive," p. 45.

to be linked, or closely related, to the decision to transition to nuclear operations.

> The shifting of efforts from one axis to another and the reinforcing of particular troop groupings began to be achieved primarily by the rapid retargeting of missile means employing nuclear warheads. However, in many cases, this alone may be insufficient. Therefore, in the course of an attack, as a rule the maneuver of nuclear blows began to be combined with the maneuver of men and weapons, including the second echelons.[78]

Thus, the most favorable time to commit the second echelon forces might well be coincident with the decision to transition to nuclear operations. As stated in *Voyennaya mysl'*:

> . . . the commitment to combat of the reserves (second echelon), as is known, is one of the culminating moments of the operation.[79]

Soviet assessments of NATO strategy and their estimates with respect to the time when NATO is most likely to initiate nuclear operations constitute the third critical factor. As mentioned above, the Soviets wish to be the first to initiate nuclear warfare. Since NATO is seen as most likely to go nuclear at the time a Soviet breakthrough seems imminent, the anticipation of the occurrence of such a time will be crucial for the Soviets. This factor reinforces the preceding two items regarding a likely "most favorable time" for transition.

The last major item likely to enter into the Soviet decision-making process is the Soviet leadership's assessment of the correlation of forces expected to prevail following the exchange of nuclear strikes (rather than the correlation existing at the beginning of the war). Statements on the calculation of the correlation of forces and its practical use abound in the Soviet and East European military literature, with great importance placed on the military correlation, particularly in terms of nuclear weapons. The correlation of forces calculation takes into account numerous operational factors, including the status and readiness of all

---

78. Savkin, *Basic Principles of Operational Art and Tactics*, p. 170.

79. Col. V. Bilaonov and Col. I. Kabachevskiy, "Air Defense of Ground Troops in Offensive Operations," *Voyennaya mysl'*, No. 10, October 1966, FPIR 0504/67, May 29, 1967, p. 48.

Transition to Nuclear Operations 49

Warsaw Pact nuclear delivery units, the availability of intelligence on NATO nuclear targets, the Warsaw Pact attack strategy, and NATO capabilities and assessed strategy for attacking Warsaw Pact units in response. The enemy is assumed to act reasonably and in his (NATO's) best interest. If the effect of the exchange as calculated would not result in a significant nuclear advantage for the Soviet Union, then the time may not be favorable for a strike. On the other hand, if it appears that the strike would result in a significant, and maximum, improvement for the Soviets in the correlation of forces, then a decision to initiate nuclear operations would be substantiated.

Three interesting insights can be gleaned from this approach. First, there is an enormous incentive on the part of the Soviet Union to forestall NATO dispersal of its nuclear weapons and to strike when the locations of those weapons are all well known—that is, at the very beginning of the war, *if NATO has not dispersed*. Second, the Soviet prognostication of the correlation of forces will be most significantly affected by Soviet reconnaissance of NATO targets and by the viability of NATO's Command, Control, Communications, and Intelligence (C^3I). Two Soviet activities in the initial phase of the war, therefore, will be to conduct, as continuously as possible, reconnaissance on all NATO nuclear targets, and to destroy, in addition to NATO nuclear weapons, all related NATO C^3I capabilities. Third, if the initial phase—with its major efforts directed against NATO's nuclear capabilities (which include command, control, and reconnaissance capabilities)—were to be particularly successful, then the correlation of forces would already have changed. In such a case, a Soviet decision to use nuclear weapons might well be viewed as counterproductive, since it would not significantly improve the correlation of forces and, in addition, would risk triggering an intercontinental nuclear exchange. As argued earlier in this paper, the literature examined has yielded no evidence that the Soviets are interested in keeping the war conventional. However, if it is assumed that this course remains a possibility for the Soviets, then attention paid to their view of the correlation of forces may make it possible to determine what level of damage inflicted by non-nuclear Soviet actions against NATO's nuclear capabilities (including C^3I and reconnaissance) would be sufficient to cause the ratio of the initial correlation of forces to the maximum correlation of forces after the exchange to drop below unity.

Still, the mere fact that a Soviet conventional attack proves successful in some sense is, in itself, no reason to expect that the Soviets will not go nuclear. Because of their emphasis on achieving surprise in their initial nuclear strike, a successful conventional phase attack might lead the Soviets to accelerate rather than delay the introduction of nuclear weapons, so as to be sure to achieve surprise. Consider, for example, the following quotation taken from an article specifically focused on the conventional phase, written during the time when the Soviets are believed to have been initially formulating their basic strategy on transitioning:

> The successful beginning and development of combat operations by conventional means of destruction by one of the sides [USSR] and the quickly growing danger of use of nuclear weapons by the other side [NATO] might force the one side [USSR] to abandon operations only by conventional means considerably before it succeeds in resolving the outlined minimum of missions despite the favorable premises for this. Finally, the duration of operations with the use of just conventional means can be sharply decreased for the purpose of achieving greater surprise of a nuclear strike and faster destruction of the enemy.[80]

This statement points to the possibility that the deciding criterion with respect to the timing of transition is not the success of the front line assault on NATO defense positions, but rather the attack on NATO nuclear forces that also would be initiated at the very beginning of the war. The success of this latter attack would be evaluated according to the correlation of forces calculation technique.

Further, the Soviets—to the extent they would be interested in shifting the correlation of forces sufficiently in their favor so as to obviate the need to initiate nuclear operations—might consider employing chemical munitions. The Soviets may well view chemical weapons as intermediate between conventional and nuclear weapons, and they may not hesitate to use them in a conventional phase to achieve their objectives. That the Soviets consider such weapons to fall in an intermediate category is suggested by a) a 1969 quotation in *Voyennaya mysl'* referring to a dated (1963) comment by then-U.S. Director, Defense Research and Engineering Harold Brown to the effect that the United States considered chemical munitions as intermediate between conven-

---

80. Samorukov, "Combat Operations Involving Conventional Means of Destruction," p. 30.

Transition to Nuclear Operations 51

tional and nuclear weapons,[81] and b) by the enormous growth in chemical warfare capabilities achieved by the Soviets since the late 1960s.[82] Consideration of the role of chemical weapons in the conventional phase is particularly interesting because they are much more effective than conventional munitions for the mission areas most critical to the Soviets in that phase: i.e., preventing the movement of NATO reserves, attacking NATO anti-tank defenses, rendering NATO nuclear storage areas and airbase facilities inoperable, and destroying NATO command and control. NATO's lack of attention to chemical warfare preparedness has heightened its vulnerability in this regard and has provided an incentive for the Soviets to employ chemical weapons massively to achieve their principal objectives very early in the war.

However, it is possible that such weapons might not be used in the very first strike. The Soviets may well believe that immediate use of chemical weapons would make a NATO nuclear use more likely. Holding off for a short time might prove advantageous to the Soviet cause, since the fog and confusion of war could cover the mass application of chemical weapons, thus greatly enhancing the surprise factor and possibly reducing the likelihood of an automatic U.S. response. Waiting a few hours before initiating the use of chemical munitions would also facilitate the insertion of behind-the-lines assault units. At the same time, it is difficult to envision that the Soviets could accomplish their objectives as quickly as they desire while limiting themselves to the employment of just conventional capabilities. Consequently—and particularly if the Soviets should be interested in reducing the requirement to go nuclear—their incentive to use chemical weapons massively throughout NATO forward deployment and rear areas will be substantial.

Considerations of Self-Deterrence

One of the dominant Western beliefs regarding nuclear war is that it would result in almost overpowering damage; hence, the need to delay

---

81. "The Secret Arsenal of the USA," *Voyennaya mysl'*, No. 6, June 1969, FPD 0008/70, January 30, 1970, p. 102.
82. Amoretta M. Hoeber and Joseph D. Douglass, Jr., "The Neglected Threat of Chemical Warfare," *International Security*, Vol. 3, No. 1, Summer 1978.

the nuclear decision and prolong the conventional phase is imperative. This appears, however, to be solely a Western assumption, and reflects consideration of neither the military or political objectives of the Soviet Union nor the Soviet approach to controlling damage.

Soviet military doctrine and strategy are, first and foremost, offensive. Their objective in the event of war in Europe is to move in and occupy the subcontinent as rapidly and efficiently as possible, making maximum effective use of all political and military capabilities. This is applicable to both a war confined to the European theater of operations and a worldwide nuclear conflict. In each case the Soviet goal is victory; and to achieve victory, it is essential to occupy rather than destroy the territory, install governments that are favorable to communism, and exploit available resources.

The following paragraph—which appeared at the beginning of a *Voyennaya mysl'* article concerned with the effectiveness of strategic bombing in World War II and the application to modern-day situations of lessons learned during that war—reflects the relevant basic political guidance:

> In the past if one of the warring countries, in planning military actions, counted upon quickly destroying the enemy army, seizing his vitally important areas and driving any particular state out of the war, it did not attempt to destroy the industrial installations. On the contrary, it was interested in preserving them for the support of its own troops and the entire country. In such a case, air attacks and others means of destruction were directed only against those targets which, during the planned period of military operations, provided the enemy with the greatest capability for active resistance. This proposition is confirmed by numerous examples.[83]

In the event of a war, Soviet thinking clearly calls for minimizing the destruction of those assets they wish to capture, and focusing their efforts against those targets that would provide the greatest resistance during the planned period of the war (which is probably measured in days). The importance of limiting the destruction of industrial areas has

---

83. Col. M. Shirokov, "The Question of Influences on the Military and Economic Potential of Warring States," *Voyennaya mysl'*, No. 4, April 1968, FPD 0052/69, May 27, 1969, p. 33.

been set forth in several places in the Soviet literature. The main historical example cited in support of this concept is the USSR's seizure of the Polish Silesian industrial district in World War II, which was accomplished without causing damage. This particular example is interesting in a second regard, as well, for it demonstrates that the concept of limiting damage to valuable territory in no way implies that the opposing military forces are not to be defeated and destroyed. Quite the contrary was the case: a corridor was provided in the engagement to allow the enemy forces to withdraw from the region; following their withdrawal, they were destroyed.[84]

When considering the Soviet interest in leaving intact, to the extent possible, areas which are seized, it is important not to confuse Soviet morality with Western morality, nor Soviet assessments of what is valuable with Western assessments. The Soviet concern over damage appears to be focused on physical—rather than human—destruction; they seem concerned with human destruction only to the extent that it might lead to troubles within the Soviet Army associated with the specter of cleaning up hundreds of thousands of bodies, or might promote the development of a highly motivated indigenous movement against the Soviets in their rear. Such worries do not mean that a given target will be spared—only that weapons other than massive nuclear ones might well be used.

> Political motives can force the abandonment of strikes against extremely important economic and military targets *or* their implementation *with smaller forces and means and on a selective basis.*[85]

And:

> . . . at present political conditions will be considered when selecting regions for delivering nuclear strikes on a country-wide scale and when determining the number of objectives, the priority of inflicting strikes, and the

---

84. Col. G. Yefimov, "The Role of Cities in Armed Combat," *Voyennaya mysl'*, No. 3, March 1971, FPD 0020, March 24, 1974, p. 68; and *Dictionary of Basic Military Terms*, p. 256.

85. Shirokov, "The Question of Influences on the Military and Economic Potential of Warring States," p. 39. (Emphasis added.)

methods of destruction of industrial, administrative-political and other centers.[86]

Two of these methods are of particular interest. The first is the use of assault forces, for which air bases constitute a class of targets of particular importance. For example:

> A favorable result from the operations of a tank group in combat with operational defense reserves depends to a great extent on effective and continuous fighter aircraft and antiaircraft missile cover of its marching columns and combat formations. The seizure and holding of airfields and landing strips deep within enemy defenses aid the aircraft supporting the tank group.[87]

The second method of special interest is the use of chemical weapons, as briefly discussed above. The Soviets appear to view chemical weapons as particularly effective in attacks on cities and industrial areas.[88]

A third possible approach has been discussed in the context of Warsaw Pact plans for attacking Britain.[89] An initial Soviet objective in any attack would be to disorganize and disrupt military and political control so as to disable the enemy's capability to mount an effective, organized defense or counterattack. In the case of Britain, an important target for this purpose would be the Houses of Parliament. However, to destroy these buildings by bombing is considered counterproductive, in view of their symbolic importance; destruction of the Houses, it is thought, might unite the British against the Soviets, including even the "progressive factions" that are important in the Soviet plans for postwar occupation and control. An alternative which apparently has been

---

86. *Ibid.*
87. Lt. Gen. (Res) B. Arushanyan, "Combat Operations by Tank Units Against Operational Defense Resources," *Voyennaya mysl'*, No. 1, January 1966, FDD 966, August 23, 1966, p. 34.
88. C.N. Donnelly, "Soviet Techniques for Combat in Built-Up Areas," *International Defense Review*, February 1977; and C.N. Donnelly, "Fighting in Built-Up Areas: a Soviet View—Part II," *RUSI Journal*, July 1977.
89. Interviews with a former East European senior officer, October–December, 1978.

Transition to Nuclear Operations

considered entails poisoning the water supply in the residential areas where most of the bourgeois leaders reside; disrupting the London Underground subway system, thus effectively snarling transportation in the city; and seizing communication facilities. In this way, Soviet aims could be achieved without stimulating the potential backlash mentioned above. Czech military intelligence is credited with having a major role in both the planning of these types of measures and their potential implementation throughout Great Britain on the eve of the war.

Furthermore, the Soviet approach to assessing damage is believed to be one of examining ratios rather than absolute numbers. In other words, what would be of prime concern to the Soviets would be the relative—not the total—damage done to the European subcontinent. An attack that destroyed ten percent of the population and industrial resources might well sound unthinkable in absolute quantities; however, when a fractional approach is utilized, such damage might be considered relatively trivial in comparison with the value obtained. Additionally, it should be noted that during World War II many physical assets (including tools and machinery that Western society might have considered destroyed and useless) were salvaged by the Soviets and shipped back to the Soviet Union. Their threshold of salvage value is probably considerably below that of Western countries.

Thus, when the Soviets refer to the avoidance of collateral damage—as in the quotations cited above—what is principally meant is the preservation of assets in which the Soviet Union has a special political, economic, or military interest. As one of the present authors has explained in an earlier paper,[90] the Soviets would like:

> . . . to be able to use in one's own interest the military-political, military-economic, military-geographic and directly operational-strategic elements characteristic of this or that theater.[91]

Samorukov has further explained the Soviet motivation as follows:

> The destructive nature of modern warfare, the difficulty of transporting material means from the depth of a country and the great vulnerability of rear

---

90. J.D. Douglass, Jr., "Soviet Nuclear Strategy in Europe: A Selective Targeting Doctrine," *Strategic Review*, Vol. 5, No. 4 (Fall 1977).

91. Arushanyan, "Combat Operations by Tank Units Against Operational Defense Resources," p. 15.

area organs make it necessary to devote serious attention to a study of the possibilities for acquiring local resources in theaters of military operations.

For this purpose, it is very important to determine which targets and enemy regions should be left intact or rapidly reconstructed and used in the interests of strengthening the economic potential of our own country and for supplying the troops.

It is important to determine which, what, where and in what quantity the local resources can be stored and used in the interests of the troops. It is important also to determine what are the conditions for acquiring or using local resources (the presence of electric-power and transport means, manpower resources, transport capability, etc.).[92]

In addition to industrial areas, the Soviets are concerned about collateral damage to such assets as transportation lines and marshalling yards. Discussion has also been identified in the Soviet literature regarding the use of multiple small yields against area targets such as airbases, so as to reduce physical destruction and radioactive contamination.

The Soviets also recognize the difficulties posed by nuclear weapons for ground force operations. Problems often explicitly cited in the Soviet literature include fire, flood, radioactive contamination, and rubble.

The fact is that the use of means of mass destruction has caused the appearance of a number of factors which hinder and, in a number of cases, preclude the conduct of troop maneuver. Included among them, for example, is the presence of broad zones of radioactive contamination, regions of solid destruction, fires, flooding, etc., which occur as the result of nuclear strikes.[93]

All of these effects—if they were to occur—would impede ground force operations, and the Soviets recognize the need to take them carefully into account in planning nuclear strikes. It has even been suggested that, within the Front area, the commander of ground forces likely to encounter these problems should have the responsibility of determining

---

92. Samorukov, "Combat Operations Involving Conventional Means of Destruction," pp. 60–61.

93. Col. V. Kyznetsov and Col. B. Andreyev, "Coordination Between Aviation and Tanks," *Voyennaya mysl'*, No. 8, August 1966, FPD 0761/67, August 7, 1967, p. 45.

Transition to Nuclear Operations

what targets should be struck and what yields should be used in the process.

It is not precluded that surface nuclear bursts can be planned against *deep* objectives, but it must be very well planned as to what kind and where (along the path of tank forces), inasmuch as this may create zones of radioactive contamination, destruction, inundation and fires.

It is considered best for the commander of tank forces to decide all questions of nuclear weapons employment immediately within the zone of advance of tank groupings to the depth of missile range. He will probably have to determine the target, types, methods and time of delivery of nuclear strikes both for his own missiles and for the carrier aircraft operating in the zone of advance.[94]

In this connection, as suggested in the following definitions from the Soviet dictionary of military terms, high-altitude bursts would be appropriate for use against several target classes, and would be exploded at altitudes that would produce no fallout contamination:

VYSOKIY VOZDUSHNYY YADERNYY VZRYV [high altitude nuclear burst]—An explosion at a height for which radioactive contamination of the locality in the vicinity of ground zero is negligible. Contamination in the wake of the cloud may be disregarded. It is expedient to use a high altitude nuclear burst to destroy troops without cover and to demolish objectives having limited structural strength. Such an explosion may also be used against troops located in very simple cover.[95]

VYSOTNYY YADERNYY VZRYV [high altitude nuclear burst]—A nuclear explosion detonated high enough to be harmless at ground level, for the purpose of destroying the means of air attack (aircraft, missiles).[96]

Another element which must be noted in assessing the Soviet interest in limiting damage concerns the possibility that the USSR might utilize high yields (several hundred kilotons) on tactical (FROG) and operational-tactical (SCUD) missiles. The use of high yields and the interest in limiting damage are not necessarily inconsistent. The impor-

---

94. *Ibid.*, p. 49.
95. *Dictionary of Basic Military Terms*, p. 53.
96. *Ibid.*, p. 54.

tant point is that their writings seem to indicate that the Soviets believe nuclear weapons can be used effectively without destroying the prize that Europe represents. It is recognized that the use of such weapons would cause considerable damage—but the degree of damage expected is not so high that the Soviets would be self-deterred from using nuclear weapons, as has been suggested by several high-level Western defense officials and civilian analysts. What does emerge from the Soviet literature is a focus on employments that are militarily effective and politically meaningful. The references above to the use of high-altitude bursts to destroy troops without causing any militarily appreciable contamination may provide one of the explanations for the usefulness of some high-yield FROG and SCUD weapons.

Escalation Flexibility

A concomitant dimension of the Soviet commitment to control and war-fighting rather than massive retaliation can be seen in the form which their mass initial nuclear strike would take, and in their interest in command (weapon employment) flexibility. Although the Soviets seem to place considerable emphasis on the simultaneity of the various components of the initial nuclear strike, one must be careful not to read too much into this. Simultaneity is important insofar as surprise is concerned; all targets should be hit at once so that no targets have time to disperse following recognition that the attack has commenced. However, the Soviet approach also incorporates the sequencing of strikes. It is recognized that not all targets will be available at the same time; hence, it will be necessary to prepare several salvos of strikes separated by enough time to allow for both tactical and strategic strike reconnaissance and the reloading of missiles. As seen from an operational- tactical perspective, in the case of air power

> . . . considerable influence on the degree of simultaneous massed employment of air power is exerted by the properties of the intended targets, the majority of which are mobile. For this reason, for example, front-attached aircraft cannot attack only on the basis of preliminary data on the character and location of targets. A certain number of aircraft must be assigned to target search as well as patrol. This stretches out the time of attack and limits subsequent massed employment.[97]

---

97. Bryuklanov, "The Massed Employment of Aircraft," p. 47.

Transition to Nuclear Operations

Where there are limitations on the capability to execute a mass, simultaneous attack, the target priorities for the Soviets are NATO nuclear means and, at the operational-tactical level, main NATO defense groupings:

> However it is not always possible to inflict a simultaneous and decisive defeat due to a lack of weapons, particularly nuclear ammunition. Consequently, the defeat of an enemy before he can launch his attack should be carried out in a selective manner. During this period of destruction, involving the use of nuclear weapons and strikes by artillery, air units and other weapons, prime attention should be given to the destruction of the enemy's nuclear-missile weapons, which could have an effect on defense and also to the first echelons of his grouping, which are either prepared for an offensive or have already commenced one. The fire weapons, second echelons and reserves of the attacking enemy, situated in the rear areas and not exerting any pressure on the defense at this time, should subsequently be destroyed as they advance towards the region of combat operations.[98]

This is also the "preferred" approach in support of battlefield operations. The Soviets recognize that a simultaneous strike against all enemy ground forces is not advisable, since the Soviet forces will not be able or ready to exploit the results of all the strikes at once. To obtain maximum effect from a nuclear strike against defending ground troops, the Soviet forces should be in a position such that they are able to capitalize on and exploit the shock or psychological effect of the explosion, in addition to exploiting the physical damage. Hence, when strikes against ground forces are mounted, they should be targeted against those forces that the Soviets are directly confronting.

Soviet plans and capabilities for the employment of nuclear weapons in sequenced strikes are designed with survivability and flexibility foremost in mind. Flexibility is of particular importance in this regard, and focuses on the ability to be highly selective with respect to the areas in which nuclear weapons will be employed, the missions to be undertaken, and the redirection of strikes in the course of combat operations. The need for flexibility is consistently emphasized throughout the Soviet literature. Two types of flexibility are examined in these discussions: flexibility prior to the start of the war (the development of options

---

98. Solov'yev and Taran, "The Employment of Defense by the Ground Forces under Modern Conditions," p. 49.

or variations in plans), and flexibility during the war (changes in plans and retargeting). For example:

> ... flexibility in the increase in efforts is the second important requirement. It consists of a strictly definite utilization (in accordance with the conditions) of the various forces and means used for the increase in effort. Here, we should consider two aspects, i.e., the ability of the commanders and the staffs to abandon quickly and decisively the previously adopted plan for the increase in efforts, in conformity with the rapidly and abruptly altering conditions and the skillful employment of the arsenal of forces and means (much greater than in the past), permitting a variation in their employment.[99]

The ability to change plans and retarget nuclear strikes is especially stressed in the Soviet literature.

> Operational maneuver is usually carried out in accordance with the plan and under the leadership of the command element of the corresponding large units. It must insure the successful achievement of the goal of the operation or fulfillment of its intermediate missions. The main content of operational maneuver is the redirection of nuclear strikes inflicted by operational-tactical rockets and by rocket-carrying aircraft of frontal aviation, as well as the shifting of groupings of troops for the purpose of the maximum exploitation subsequently of the results of nuclear strikes.[100]

The need for considerable flexibility in shifting efforts from one area to another also is emphasized. Included in this regard is the possibility of concentrating strikes principally in either the tactical area or the operational-strategic area, depending on the needs of the battle.

> A highly centralized control combined with one-man command and the granting of extensive initiative to subordinates enables our command personnel to maneuver troop groupings quickly and flexibility to create the desired balance of forces on selected axes effectively and to organize necessary coordination between them in short periods of time.[101]

---

99. Col. D. Samorukov and Col. L. Semeyko, "The Increase of Efforts in Nuclear Warfare Operations," *Voyennaya mysl'*, No. 10, October 1968, FPD 0084/69, August 29, 1969, p. 52.

100. Begunov, "The Maneuver of Forces and Material in an Offensive," p. 45.

101. Tyushkevich, "The Methodology for the Correlation of Forces in War," p. 35.

Transition to Nuclear Operations

The significance of flexibility is especially prominent in Soviet discussions of superiority and its benefits. For example, as stated in *Voyennaya mysl'* in 1969:

> . . . first and foremost account should be taken of the fact that the established correlation of forces determines the actual capabilities of the sides to exert influence on one another at a given moment with a determined degree of probability of success. In the process the advantage in principle accrues to that side which significantly surpasses the other in strength in the aggregate or in individual and the more essential components of combat might. Superiority accelerates the process of the physical and moral defeat of the enemy, makes it possible to operate more daringly and decisively, and to impose one's will on the enemy and to attack him more successfully. It promotes the development of flexibility in the selection of scales, forms and methods of conducting combat operations, expands the scope of methods for coordinating the delivery of nuclear, fire and air attacks with the maneuver of troops, and increases the effectiveness of using space, time, and other factors which influence the course of military operations. Conversely, an obvious shortage of forces substantially limits capabilities for organizing the repulsing of the enemy.[102]

NATO discussions tend to identify categories which are relatively similar to those utilized by the Soviets—i.e., battlefield (tactical), selected interdiction (operational-tactical), and regional (strategic). There exist major differences in approach, however. When NATO discussions focus on a restricted or limited employment option with respect to the use of nuclear weapons, such employment tends to occur in the battlefield category. In contrast, in the Soviet literature such employment tends to refer to the deep strike. The "strategic" component almost always is present; the main question is whether or not short-range systems will be used near the forward edge of the battle area (FEBA). As stated in *The Offensive:*

> In those instances where *podrazdeleniya* are conducting combat operations and nuclear weapons *are not* employed or *are employed to a limited extent and chiefly against deep objectives,* it is advantageous for penetration into the depth of the enemy defense to use intervals and gaps in its deployment,

---

102. *Ibid.*, p. 32.

the flanks of troop groupings, and sectors occupied by the enemy with a light density of men and material.[103]

This notion also appears in an earlier *Voyennaya mysl'* article:

> The scale and consequences of strikes against objectives in the deep strategic rear may significantly exceed the strikes against troop groupings in the theaters of military operations.[104]

In the Soviet military dictionary, "deap rear" is defined as follows:

> GLUBOKIY TYL [deep rear]—That part of the territory of a state (or states) beyond the range of enemy operational and tactical means of attack. Under conditions of nuclear-missile warfare, the basic elements of the enemy deep rear may include: the economic base of the war; the governmental and supreme command systems; and the strategic nuclear weapons of an armed conflict.[105]

Thus, in the previous quote, "deep strategic rear" could include the United States and might also encompass that area of NATO beyond the reach of operational-tactical missiles. If the breakthrough operations were going reasonably well, for example, it might be considered best to employ the operational-strategic capabilities only against NATO reserves and NATO nuclear forces. This would greatly reduce the problem of coordinating nuclear strikes with the ground force operations that were spearheading the breakthrough and developing its success. Additionally, such a course would allow the transition to nuclear warfare to be accomplished more swiftly and with greater surprise.

On the other hand, if the attack were to begin with a surprise nuclear strike (that is, before the first echelon forces had moved forward and engaged NATO forward defense or security forces), then—from the operations point of view—the nuclear strikes should be launched against the NATO forward defense and security forces. As explained in *The Offensive:*

---

103. Sidorenko, *The Offensive,* p. 89. (Emphasis added.)
104. Shirokov, "The Question of Influences on the Military and Economic Potential of Warring States," p. 33.
105. *Dictionary of Basic Military Terms,* p. 60.

Transition to Nuclear Operations

... depending on the concept of the battle, the method for the troops to launch the offensive, and the distance of the attack position from the enemy FEBA, the nuclear strikes are launched against objectives located on the defender's FEBA or in the depth of his disposition.[106]

In Soviet military science, variations in types, forms, and scales of nuclear employment are believed to be mostly a function (aside from political factors) of the time when the war becomes nuclear, and of the targets acquired, confirmed, and not yet destroyed by other means. To the extent that geography plays a role, the only evident distinction is between strikes in the deep rear and strikes in the tactical depth. In the Soviet view, strikes in the tactical depth may be withheld or delayed. The possibility of withholding deep strikes also is implicit in Soviet military writings; it is believed, however, that the Soviets would most likely view this option as applying to a variant wherein the West would engage first in a limited nuclear strike and the USSR would temporarily respond in kind—thus misleading NATO while better preparing to launch an all-out nuclear attack throughout the depth of the theater.

---

106. Sidorenko, *The Offensive,* p. 115.

National Strategy Information Center, Inc.

PUBLICATIONS

Frank N. Trager, Editor
Dorothy E. Nicolosi, Associate Editor
Joyce E. Larson, Managing Editor

STRATEGY PAPERS

Conventional War and Escalation: The Soviet View by Joseph D. Douglass, Jr. and Amoretta M. Hoeber, November 1981

Soviet Perceptions of Military Doctrine and Military Power: The Interaction of Theory and Practice by John J. Dziak, June 1981

How Little is Enough? SALT and Security in the Long Run by Francis P. Hoeber, January 1981

Raw Material Supply in a Multipolar World by Yuan-li Wu, October 1973. Revised edition, October 1979

India: Emergent Power? by Stephen P. Cohen and Richard L. Park, June 1978

The Kremlin and Labor: A Study in National Security Policy by Roy Godson, November 1977

The Evolution of Soviet Security Strategy 1965–1975 by Avigdor Haselkorn, November 1977

The Geopolitics of the Nuclear Era by Colin S. Gray, September 1977

The Sino-Soviet Confrontation: Implications for the Future by Harold C. Hinton, September 1976 (Out of print)

Food, Foreign Policy, and Raw Materials Cartels by William Schneider, Jr., February 1976

Strategic Weapons: An Introduction by Norman Polmar, October 1975 (Out of print)

Soviet Sources of Military Doctrine and Strategy by William F. Scott, July 1975

Detente: Promises and Pitfalls by Gerald L. Steibel, March 1975 (Out of print)

Oil, Politics and Sea Power: The Indian Ocean Vortex by Ian W.A.C. Adie, December 1974 (Out of print)

The Soviet Presence in Latin America by James D. Theberge, June 1974

The Horn of Africa by J. Bowyer Bell, Jr., December 1973

Research and Development and the Prospects for International Security by Frederick Seitz and Rodney W. Nichols, December 1973

The People's Liberation Army: Communist China's Armed Forces by Angus M. Fraser, August 1973 (Out of print)

Nuclear Weapons and the Atlantic Alliance by Wynfred Joshua, May 1973 (Out of print)

How to Think About Arms Control and Disarmament by James E. Dougherty, May 1973 (Out of print)

The Military Indoctrination of Soviet Youth by Leon Goure, January 1973 (Out of print)

The Asian Alliance: Japan and United States Policy by Franz Michael and Gaston J. Sigur, October 1972 (Out of print)

Iran, the Arabian Peninsula, and the Indian Ocean by R. M. Burrell and Alvin J. Cottrell, September 1972 (Out of print)

Soviet Naval Power: Challenge for the 1970s by Norman Polmar, April 1972. Revised edition, September 1974 (Out of print)

How Can We Negotiate with the Communists? by Gerald L. Steibel, March 1972 (Out of print)

Soviet Political Warfare Techniques, Espionage and Propaganda in the 1970s by Lyman B. Kirkpatrick, Jr., and Howland H. Sargeant, January 1972 (Out of print)

The Soviet Presence in the Eastern Mediterranean by Lawrence L. Whetten, September 1971 (Out of print)

The Military Unbalance: Is the U.S. Becoming a Second Class Power? June 1971 (Out of print)

The Future of South Vietnam by Brigadier F. P. Serong, February 1971 (Out of print)

Strategy and National Interests: Reflections for the Future by Bernard Brodie, January 1971 (Out of print)

The Mekong River: A Challenge in Peaceful Development for Southeast Asia by Eugene R. Black, December 1970 (Out of print)

Problems of Strategy in the Pacific and Indian Oceans by George C. Thomson, October 1970 (Out of print)

Soviet Penetration into the Middle East by Wynfred Joshua, July 1970. Revised edition, October 1971 (Out of print)

Australian Security Policies and Problems by Justus M. van der Kroef, May 1970 (Out of print)

Detente: Dilemma or Disaster? by Gerald L. Steibel, July 1969 (Out of print)

The Prudent Case for Safeguard by William R. Kintner, June 1969 (Out of print)

AGENDA PAPERS

The China Sea: The American Stake in its Future by Harold C. Hinton, January 1981

NATO, Turkey, and the Southern Flank: A Mideastern Perspective by Ihsan Gürkan, March 1980

The Soviet Threat to NATO's Northern Flank by Marian K. Leighton, November 1979

Does Defense Beggar Welfare? Myths Versus Realities by James L. Clayton, June 1979 (Out of print)

Naval Race or Arms Control in the Indian Ocean? (Some Problems in Negotiating Naval Limitations) by Alvin J. Cottrell and Walter F. Hahn, September 1978 (Out of print)

Power Projection: A Net Assessment of U.S. and Soviet Capabilities by W. Scott Thompson, April 1978

Understanding the Soviet Military Threat, How CIA Estimates Went Astray by William T. Lee, February 1977 (Out of print)

Toward a New Defense for NATO, The Case for Tactical Nuclear Weapons, July 1976 (Out of print)

Seven Tracks to Peace in the Middle East by Frank R. Barnett, April 1975

Arms Treaties with Moscow: Unequal Terms Unevenly Applied? by Donald G. Brennan, April 1975 (Out of print)

Toward a U.S. Energy Policy by Klaus Knorr, March 1975 (Out of print)

Can We Avert Economic Warfare in Raw Materials? US Agriculture as a Blue Chip by William Schneider, Jr., July 1974

BOOKS

Arms, Men, and Military Budgets: Issues for Fiscal Year 1981 by Francis P. Hoeber, William Schneider, Jr., Norman Polmar, and Ray Bessette, May 1980

Arms, Men, and Military Budgets: Issues for Fiscal Year 1979 by Francis P. Hoeber, David B. Kassing, and William Schneider, Jr., February 1978

Arms, Men, and Military Budgets: Issues for Fiscal Year 1978 edited by Francis P. Hoeber and William Schneider, Jr., May 1977

Arms, Men, and Military Budgets: Issues for Fiscal Year 1977 edited by William Schneider, Jr., and Francis P. Hoeber, May 1976 (Out of print)

* * *

Intelligence Requirements for the 1980s: Counterintelligence (Volume III of a Series) edited by Roy Godson, January 1981

Intelligence Requirements for the 1980s: Analysis and Estimates (Volume II of a Series) edited by Roy Godson, June 1980

Intelligence Requirements for the 1980s: Elements of Intelligence (Volume I of a Series) edited by Roy Godson, October 1979

* * *

U.S. Policy and Low-Intensity Conflict: Potentials for Military Struggles in the 1980s edited by Sam C. Sarkesian and William L. Scully, June 1981

New Foundations for Asian and Pacific Security edited by Joyce E. Larson, September 1980

The Fateful Ends and Shades of SALT: Past . . . Present . . . And Yet to Come? by Paul H. Nitze, James E. Dougherty, and Francis X. Kane, March 1979

Strategic Options for the Early Eighties: What Can Be Done? edited by William R. Van Cleave and W. Scott Thompson, February 1979

Oil, Divestiture and National Security edited by Frank N. Trager, December 1976 (Out of print)

Indian Ocean Naval Limitations, Regional Issues and Global Implications by Alvin J. Cottrell and Walter F. Hahn, April 1976